NAZI GERMANY

UNIFORM WITH THIS BOOK

RONALD HINGLEY *Russian Revolution*

IN PREPARATION
LOIS MITCHISON *Red China*

A BODLEY HEAD CONTEMPORARY HISTORY

NAZI GERMANY

RICHARD PROCKTOR

THE BODLEY HEAD

LONDON SYDNEY

TORONTO

ISBN 0 370 01550 9
© Richard Procktor 1970
Maps © The Bodley Head Ltd 1970
Printed and bound in Great Britain for
The Bodley Head
9 Bow Street, London WC 2
by William Clowes & Sons, Beccles
Set in Monotype Baskerville
First published 1970

CONTENTS

ACKNOWLEDGMENTS

Thanks are due to the following for permission to use copyright photographs: the Imperial War Museum, pages 13, 14, 19, 20 and 21, 22, 27, 53, 85, 89, 92, 96, 100, 103; the Camera Press, pages 9, 76, 80, 98; Erich Andres of Hamburg-Altona, pages 104 and 105; the Radio Times Hulton Picture Library, page 28; the Keystone Press Agency, pages 34, 37, 45, 48, 56, 61, 66, 78; and United Press International (UK) Ltd., pages 40, 64, 71.

1

The Great Power

Only since 1871 has it been possible to point on the map to a nation called Germany. In spite of this, for centuries there have been people who called themselves Germans. They possessed a few characteristics in common: they lived in Central Europe without being either Latin or Slav; they spoke the German language; above all they regarded themselves as German.

In the eighteenth century, Germany had been made up of 234 separate territorial units, ranging from states of major European significance like Prussia to tiny principalities based on one castle and a few surrounding villages. When the map of Europe was redrawn after the defeat of Napoleon Bonaparte at Waterloo in 1815, the new German Confederation still comprised thirty-nine states.

After 1815, Prussia began gradually to dominate and then to unify these German states. As compensation for the loss of the greater part of her Polish possessions to Russia, Prussia had acquired the Rhine Province. This not only gave her three million more Germans, but an area of vital strategic and economic importance in the future. In the short term, it further complicated the problems of economic administration. Prussia was faced with sixty-seven different internal tariffs and thirteen non-Prussian enclosed territories with systems of their own. The Prussian Finance Minister, Motz, devised the idea of the *Zollverein*, or Customs Union. This started by breaking down all customs barriers within Prussia in 1818. By 1829 it included seventeen states and twenty-six million people. The easing of trade within Prussia and the protection by tariffs against rivals outside the *Zollverein* led to remarkable economic expansion. Between 1834 and 1842 imports and exports doubled. A railway system developed from 282 miles in 1840 to 5,134 miles in 1850. This system was based on Berlin. Gradually the greater part of Germany became accustomed to success under Prussian leadership.

The unification of Germany was to a very large extent a personal triumph for the Prussian statesman, Otto von Bismarck. Appreciating the economic and industrial strength of Prussia and the strategic value of her railways with their capacity to mobilise armies with exceptional speed, he proceeded to exploit these advantages through ruthless diplomacy. Prussia crushed in battle between 1863 and 1870 first Denmark, then Austria, whose Habsburg Emperor had for centuries been the overlord of the German states, and finally France, previously regarded as the dominant military force on the Continent. As a symbol of spectacular conquest, on January 18th 1871, the King of Prussia William I was proclaimed the first German Emperor, or Kaiser, in the captured Palace of Versailles, where once French kings had dazzled the courts of Europe.

The constitution of the German Empire had been carefully devised by Bismarck. In order to offset the fears of the Kaiser and his *Junker* landowners, with their huge estates east of the Elbe, that national unity would involve the advance of the power of the people, Bismarck made sure that the Imperial Crown was offered by the German princes. The Bundesrat or Upper House was elected by the states. The Reichstag or Lower House was elected by universal suffrage. In practice the Bundesrat was rarely consulted and had little importance. The Reichstag could debate and confirm laws but could not introduce them. Its consent was supposed to be necessary to authorise financial measures. In fact, the revenue of the Empire (or Reich) came from customs and excise, and any deficit could be made up according to a scale of contributions from the states. Executive power lay firmly with the Kaiser and could be delegated to his two main officials, the Chancellor and the Chief of the General Staff. As long as William I was alive, this meant that effective power lay with his Chancellor, Bismarck.

Bismarck's foreign policy after 1871 was devoted to retaining the success he had already achieved. He realised that further wars were almost certain to increase hostility to Germany. He manoeuvred the chessboard of

8

diplomacy to ensure no major disturbances. As he said in 1890, 'We have annexed enough populations.'

The most spectacular of the early achievements of the German Empire were economic. Flushed by success and a war indemnity of five milliard francs from France, the German economy surged forward. The greatest triumph lay in steel production. In 1879, a London police court clerk, Thomas, and his cousin, Gilchrist, in a tiny backyard laboratory showed that phosphoric ores could be used for steel. This had great importance for Lorraine, rich in phosphoric ores and newly annexed from France. By 1914, German steel production was more than double that of Great Britain.

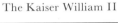

The Kaiser William II

9

Most of the wealth came into the hands of already rich industrialists organised in huge combines to control prices, known as cartels. However, wealth spread down to growing numbers of the middle classes and skilled workers. For a time Bismarck compensated these classes for their lack of power with an extensive programme of social legislation. A national standard of legal procedure, coinage and civil administration was established. Compulsory insurance for workers against sickness, accident, injury and old age was organised by the State. Liberal or Marxist Social Democrats were taught to look to the State for security if not for power.

In November 1888, William II became the new Kaiser. Unlike the ponderous soldier, William I, his grandfather, who could never forget Bismarck's service to the Crown, the new, young Emperor was impetuous and confident that he could succeed without the advice of his ageing Chancellor. The election results of 1890, which for the first time produced a majority opposed to Bismarck, provided the excuse for his dismissal.

William II took Bismarck's constitution at its face value, relegating the Chancellor to the role of adviser and taking the lead himself. He delighted in the attitudes of his grandfather and from his early years adopted a reactionary and warlike pose. His hairdresser visited him at seven o'clock each morning to train his moustache so that it bristled ferociously. He delighted in splendid uniforms. Conscious of a smattering of learning unusual among monarchs, he had a fatal facility for quickly grasping ideas without pausing to consider their implications. He pronounced often tactless judgement on every conceivable topic. In 1891, he proclaimed, 'There is only one person who is master in this Empire and I am not going to tolerate any other.' On the dismissal of Bismarck, he announced, 'The ship's course remains the same. "Full steam ahead" is the order.' There was considerable doubt whether he could understand the course. It was certain there would be plenty of steam.

The Kaiser's first efforts in foreign policy were erratic and contradictory. He replaced Bismarck with a non-political, military administrator, General von Caprivi, who was encouraged to pursue a more liberal foreign policy involving coolness towards Russia and possible friendship with Great Britain. He then appointed a rich aristocratic diplomat, Prince Chlodwig von Hohenlohe, and instructed him to reverse the policies of Caprivi. The most serious result of this phase occurred in 1895, when the Kaiser sent a telegram to Paul Kruger, President of the Transvaal, which seemed to imply that he was prepared to offer the Boers military aid against the

British. The dispatch of a strong British naval squadron to South African waters revealed Germany's inability to safeguard distant land-locked territories.

After 1900 foreign policy was more and more at the mercy of the Kaiser. The new Chancellor, Prince Bernhard von Bülow, was ideally suited to his master. He was dignified, smoothly mannered, devoid of principle and extremely anxious to please. He was nicknamed '*pomadig*', 'like hair oil'. By a series of faulty manoeuvres and alarming threats Bülow and William II decisively weakened Germany's diplomatic position.

In 1901, possible alliance with Britain was rejected. This rebuff from Germany led Britain to reconsider her relationship with France. Her traditional enemy was first charmed by King Edward VII's visit in 1903 and then persuaded to sign the '*entente cordiale*' in 1904. Anglo-French relations were still fickle but a decisive realignment had occurred. In 1905 to the amazement of Europe and of the Moroccans, the Kaiser landed at Tangier and declared himself concerned with Moroccan independence. At the ensuing Algeciras Conference, Britain firmly supported French interest in Morocco. In 1907, Great Britain and Russia settled their mutual differences in an alliance. Germany was left with Austria-Hungary as her only firm ally.

Austria viewed with concern growing nationalism in the Balkan peninsula and in particular the liberal and pro-Russian inclinations of King Peter I of Serbia. On October 6th 1908 it was announced that Austria had annexed Bosnia and Herzegovina, thus thwarting Serbian plans for expansion. In the crisis that followed, the Kaiser and von Moltke, Chief of the General Staff, firmly committed themselves to support Austria-Hungary, with force if necessary. Von Moltke wrote to his Austrian counterpart, von Hotzendorf, 'At the moment Russia mobilises, Germany will also mobilise and mobilise its entire army.'

In fairness to Bülow and the Kaiser, it is necessary to point out that their aggressive self-confidence was typical of the feelings of their most outspoken subjects. The nineties saw the spread of nationalist societies: the Colonial League, the Pan-German League and outstandingly the Navy League. In 1897 Admiral Tirpitz became Secretary of State for the Navy. Like the Kaiser, he was appalled by the insignificance of Germany's navy compared with Britain's. In 1896, Britain had 163 battleships and cruisers, Germany had ten. Tirpitz publicised the idea that with a powerful navy, Germany could become *ebenburtig*, or of equal rank with the greatest of

11

powers. He proved to be a publicist and organiser of genius. After Britain produced the ten-gun, giant battleship *The Dreadnought* in 1906, Anglo-German naval rivalry became an obsession for the nationalists of both countries. Bülow informed the Reichstag, 'We do not wish to put anyone in the shadow, but we demand our place in the sun.' The Kaiser declared, 'The trident belongs in our hands.' The Navy League gained 240,000 new members in three years.

A natural development of naval expansion and German self-esteem was the idea of being a 'world' power. For this colonies were essential. Kiao-chow in China, the Caroline, Mariana and Samoan Islands were all expensively acquired to boost prestige. The lower-middle classes, often by-passed in the race for industrial wealth, sought consolation in patriotism. Bebel, leader of the Social Democrats, who should have been following Karl Marx's instruction to prevent war by the threat of industrial strike, declared, 'If there is a war against Russia, we Socialists shall march to a man.'

In 1909, the Kaiser replaced Bülow with a mild bureaucrat, Bethman Hollweg. He felt that his own expertise would compensate for his Chancellor's inexperience in diplomacy. The results were a further incident in Morocco in 1911, which shortly afterwards became a French protectorate, and another rejection of an understanding with Britain in 1912. This was followed by an Anglo-French agreement to redeploy their fleets, the French in the Mediterranean, the British in Home Waters and the Channel. It only required a more detailed treaty between France and Russia to complete the diplomatic split into armed camps.

Renewed crisis in the Balkans developed defensive alliance into open hostility. In 1912 the Balkan states banded into a Balkan League and defeated the Turks. In the quarrel over the spoils of victory, Serbia emerged stronger and further enlarged in 1913. Flushed by victory, Serbian extremists demanded the end of Austrian rule over any Serb. Insult was followed by the outrage of the assassination of the Austrian heir on June 28th 1914 at Sarajevo, the capital of Bosnia. The Austrians issued an ultimatum to Serbia. The Serbs accepted all but one of their terms. Bethman Hollweg urged caution on the Austrians, Moltke advised action. The Russians refused to allow 'another Bosnia', and on July 30th they mobilised. On the following day Germany retaliated.

What made the Balkan issue the vital concern of Great Britain and France was the Schlieffen Plan. Chief of the General Staff from 1891 to

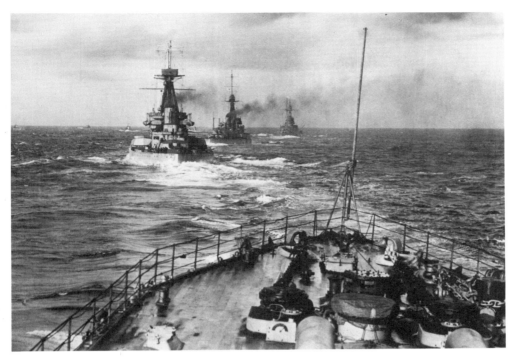

British battleships of the *Dreadnought* class

1907, von Schlieffen left as his memorial a strategic plan which made a knockout blow at France through Belgium an essential preliminary to attack on Russia. Aware of this, the English Foreign Secretary, Sir Edward Grey, offered English neutrality if Germany did not attack France. Moltke overrode the Kaiser's delight and decreed that this was impossible. Germany declared war on France on August 3rd. Britain went to war to protect Belgian neutrality on the 4th.

Bülow in his memoirs recalls asking Bethman Hollweg, 'How on earth do you think this happened?' 'Heaven knows!' was the reply.

Throughout Europe, cheering crowds greeted the outbreak of war. Among them in Munich was the son of an Austrian customs official, Adolf Hitler, who later wrote, 'For me as for every other German, the most memorable period of my life now began.'

13

2

The Collapse of
a Dream

The German General Staff, who bore such a large part of the responsibility for the declaration of war in 1914, could nevertheless view their prospects with confidence. They had just spent an extra £50,000,000 voted by the Reichstag in 1913 on improving their already formidable forces. The Kiel Canal had been opened to take their largest battleships. Their army at full mobilisation was larger than that of Russia and France put together. They held the British Expeditionary Force in such contempt that orders were given not to interfere with its transport across the Channel in order that it could be annihilated on land. The enormous howitzers produced by the Krupp and Skoda factories were the most formidable weapons in history. Above all, the generals were confident that in the Schlieffen Plan they had the blueprint of victory. The destruction of France was expected to take twenty-eight days from mobilisation at the most. Forces would be free for the Russian front by the forty-first day.

In fact to start with everything seemed to go well. The French directed their main attack towards Lorraine and were held. The Germans, first into the attack on August 5th, had seized the citadel of Liège by the 7th and then smashed its forts to pieces with their Skoda howitzers. On August 20th, von Kluck, Commander of the First Army, had captured Brussels. By the 24th the French were in retreat towards the Marne.

◄ The battlefield of Passchendaele, October 1917.
A symbol of the stagnation of the Western Front

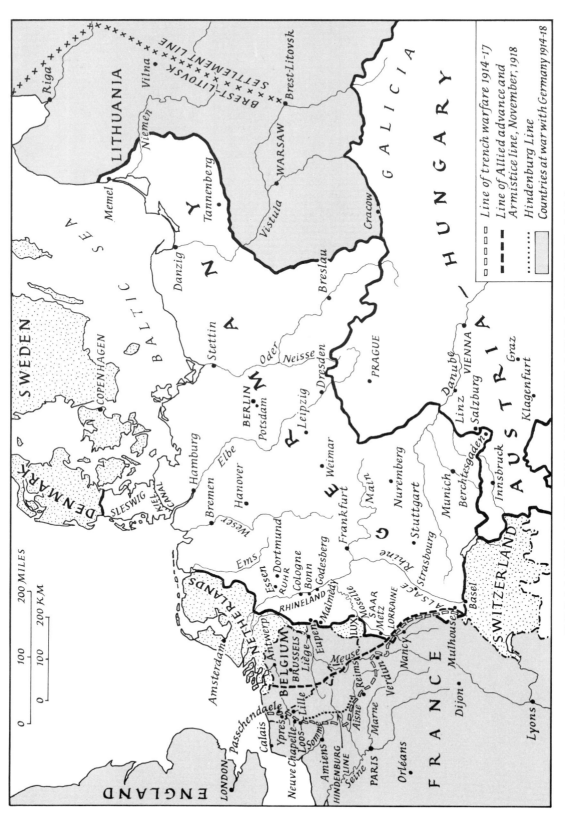

GERMANY AND HER NEIGHBOURS BEFORE 1919

Line of trench warfare 1914-17
Line of Allied advance and
Armistice line, November, 1918
Hindenburg Line
Countries at war with Germany 1914-18

ENGLAND

LONDON

NETHERLANDS

Amsterdam

BELGIUM

Antwerp
BRUSSELS
Liège
Eupen
Malmédy

RHINELAND
Essen
Dortmund
RUHR
Cologne
Bonn
Godesberg

Calais
Ypres
Loos
Lille
Neuve Chapelle
Passchendaele

Amiens
Somme
HINDENBURG
LINE

Seine
PARIS

Orléans

FRANCE

Dijon

Lyons

LUX.
Metz
LORRAINE
Moselle
SAAR

Verdun
Reims
Aisne
Marne

Nancy

Meuse

ALSACE
Strasbourg

Basel

SWITZERLAND

Mulhouse

SWEDEN

DENMARK
SLESWIG
KIEL CANAL

COPENHAGEN

BALTIC SEA

Memel

LITHUANIA

Vilna
Niemen

BREST-LITOVSK
SETTLEMENT LINE

Riga

Brest-Litovsk

Danzig

Stettin

Tannenberg

WARSAW

Vistula

POLAND

Hamburg
Bremen
Hanover
Weser
Elbe
Ems

BERLIN
Potsdam
Leipzig

Odeŕ
Neisse
Dresden

Breslau

Cracow

GALICIA

PRAGUE

GERMANY

Weimar
Frankfurt
Main
Nuremberg
Stuttgart
Munich
Berchtesgaden
Innsbruck

AUSTRIA

Linz
Salzburg
VIENNA
Graz
Klagenfurt

Danube

HUNGARY

Rhine

200 MILES
200 K.M.
100
100
0
0

On the 25th August, Moltke was so confident of success that he withdrew four divisions from his right wing, the one most essential to the encirclement of Paris, and sent them to support resistance to the Russians in the East. On the 26th, the German First Army received a severe mauling from the British at Le Cateau, and on the 30th Kluck became seriously worried about the gap developing between himself and the Second Army under General von Bülow. He now turned his army towards the east of Paris, leaving his flank exposed to an attack from Paris. On September 4th, the Military Governor of Paris, Gallieni, flung the French Sixth Army against Kluck's flank. General Joffre meanwhile began a French counter-attack towards the Marne. On September 7th, the British and the French Fifth Army advanced into the gap between Kluck and Bülow. The incredible had happened. The British and French were effectively resisting. On the 8th and 9th of September Moltke ordered withdrawal to a defensive position on the River Aisne. September 9th was the forty-first day on which all resistance should have collapsed.

Moltke's failure to win the expected victory led to his replacement by General von Falkenhayn. Falkenhayn attempted to redeem the strategic situation by striking for the Channel ports. On October 7th, the Belgians surrendered Antwerp. A fearsome battle developed round Ypres. The Kaiser appeared to witness the master-stroke. On October 31st, the Germans pierced the British line at Gheluvelt, but in a heroic counter-attack they were driven back. The Prussian Guard was finally beaten back on November 11th. The Western Front now ran from Switzerland to the North Sea. In the next three years, despite appalling bloodshed, it was not to move more than ten miles either way.

Although the Western Front was to remain the graveyard of offensives, the commanders on both sides were very slow to appreciate the situation despite terrible setbacks. By the end of 1915 the situation was abundantly clear. In March, May and September, the British and French launched fierce attacks at Neuve-Chapelle, Aubert Ridge and Loos. These attacks were based on the theory of huge numbers flung in frontal assault. In every case, German machine-gunners wrought fearful destruction. At Neuve-Chapelle a dozen German machine-guns devastated the British who had a numerical advantage of seven to one. During 1915, Falkenhayn concentrated his main efforts in the East. He restricted his Western troops to maintaining their defensive position and experimenting with poison gas near Ypres.

The main German effort to smash a hole in the Western Front was at Verdun between February and July 1916. The aim was to concentrate and annihilate the French army in an exposed salient. The result was a heroically stubborn defence led by General Pétain. 1,200 guns had been concentrated to render barely eight miles of front into a hell. Terrifying bombardment mutilated the soil but could not destroy the deeper earth-works embedded in concrete. Although the French defence was to begin with inadequate and badly organised, barbed wire and machine-gun turrets once more took their ghastly toll of troops advancing from one mud-filled shell crater to another. The German forces lost over 282,000 men to the French 315,000. Their only consolation could be that in the Allied diversionary counter-attack on the Somme from July to November 1916, the casualties were even higher. Each side lost over half a million men.

The stagnation of the Western Front was of great importance to German morale. The Germans, dreaming of the successes of 1870, had been pro-mised and expected dramatic victory. It was what they were fighting for. Furthermore the failure to annihilate France coincided with the collapse of another symbol of prestige, the colonial empire. The South African Prime Minister, Botha, crushed German resistance in South West Africa. The Japanese and Commonwealth navies gobbled up the Pacific island colonies. In December 1914 the German Pacific Fleet was destroyed almost com-pletely near the Falkland Islands. Worse still, the High Seas Fleet, brain-child of Admiral Tirpitz and above all the emblem of German might, remained largely inactive until May 1916. When a battle did develop at Jutland on May 31st and June 1st 1916, German gun-power and accuracy proved superior but not decisively so. British numbers offset heavier casualties and after August 1916, Admiral Scheer, Commander-in-Chief of the High Seas Fleet, decided against a further major battle. The Eastern Front became the only remaining focus for hopes of success.

The victories for which Germany longed in 1914 appeared in an un-expected quarter, East Prussia. It had been assumed that the lightning blow against France would be over before the Russians were fully mobilised. Urged on by the French, two Russian armies in fact began to attack on August 20th before they were fully mobilised. The attacks were directed north of the Masurian Lakes and against Tannenberg. They reduced the German Commander, Prittwitz, to hysterical panic on the telephone. Moltke acted swiftly and replaced Prittwitz by Generals Hindenburg and Ludendorff. They arrived to find an excellent and daring plan by a staff

18

German machine-gunners, destroyers of uncounted
men and traditional ideas of warfare

officer, Hoffman, already begun. The full force of the German army was to
be directed against the southern-most Russians before being concentrated
again in the north. They were greatly aided by the efficiency of the German
railway network and the Russian habit of issuing their orders uncoded over
the wireless system. Concentrated artillery wrought havoc among troops
often sharing rifles and officers without maps. The southern Russian army
was shattered. The northern army was forced into full retreat. 120,000
prisoners were taken. Germany discovered in Hindenburg and Ludendorff
the military heroes she had been looking for.

1915 and 1916 were on the whole encouraging years for the Germans.
The British attempt to outflank the Central Powers by a land-sea attack on
Gallipoli was repelled by the fierce resistance of the Turks organised by a
German military mission. German leadership was vastly superior to the
British. The Austrians who had started badly in Galicia in 1914 were re-
inforced by the Germans and a joint attack at Gorlice in 1915 turned into a

German prisoners and Canadian wounded struggle back from the front line

major triumph. In eight months the Russians were pushed back 300 miles and lost 300,000 prisoners. Further south the addition of Bulgaria to their alliance enabled the Germans and Austrians to crush Serbia. Italy and later Rumania were to join their enemies but proved to be allies of doubtful value. By the end of 1916 Rumania was reduced to the northern province of Moldavia. In October 1917 the Italians were routed at Caporetto.

In the East, by 1917 the German Army had in fact succeeded in exhausting the resources of the Russian war effort. The Russians entered the war in huge numbers. Although badly equipped, ill-fed and barely clothed, they had been united in simple devotion to their 'little father', the Tsar. By 1917 they had lost nearly 3,500,000 men. Industry and agriculture had been ruined by the war effort. Strikers had been shot down. The railway system was reduced to chaos. Desperately needed food and equipment rotted in remote sidings. The army simply wanted to stop fighting. Revolution had broken out. On March 3rd 1918, the Germans exacted a terrible peace at Brest-Litovsk. Germany annexed Poland, the Baltic Provinces, the Ukraine, Finland and the Caucasus. Most important of all, the German army

harvested in the Ukraine in 1918. A large part of the army in the East could now be transported to the West in a decisive effort to achieve a breakthrough.

The shifting fortunes of war had their effect on the domestic policies of Germany. In 1914 the Reichstag had voted the grant of war credits unanimously. The parties had declared *Burgfrieden*, a civil truce agreeing not to oppose the government. The German people were confident in their leadership and of success. They were prepared to stand the hardship of rationing. British naval blockade had caused bread to be in short supply by January 1915. '*Ersatz*' coffee made of barley, rye, chicory and figs became a national beverage. Cakes were made of clover meal and chestnut flour. Civilian clothing was rationed. Walter Rathenau, a Jewish industrialist, organised the economy for war.

By 1916 growing impatience was felt concerning the failure to achieve total victory. In August Hindenburg became Chief of the General Staff and Ludendorff his 'First Quartermaster General'. In practice the nation accepted military leadership for a military solution. The Reichstag passed a resolution expressing support for 'a peace of reconciliation', and Hinden-

German heavy gun, a combination of military
power and industrial skill

burg and Ludendorff retaliated by insisting on the Kaiser dismissing Bethman Hollweg as Chancellor. He was replaced by Ludendorff's nominee,
Michaelis, in July 1917. The future of Germany was left to Ludendorff's
military ability.

In January 1917, Ludendorff showed his mettle by demanding all-out
submarine warfare against ships trading with the Allies. The U-boats began
with spectacular success, sinking 423 Allied and neutral ships in April 1917,
but were gradually countered by the British development of the convoy
system, depth-charges and mines. The most important result was to bring
America into the war against Germany. Dramatic victory in the West
became a necessity to forestall the arrival of American equipment and men.
In March 1918 an offensive involving 2,500,000 men was launched against
the Allies. On the second day, the Germans broke through the British line
into open country. The Kaiser declared in triumph, 'The battle is won.'

The reality was different. Although the Germans captured 1,200 square
miles, the offensive began to peter out. Casualties, fatigue, lengthening lines
of communication, the awesome confusion of the old battlefields—all
played their part. To Ludendorff's horror reports began to come through of
front line troops stopping the advance to indulge in the drunken looting of
villages. The Allies united their efforts under the overall direction of the

22

French Marshal Foch. Two American generals were now included in his command. The British began to hold their line, and Ludendorff switched his main attack to the French in the Champagne district. Although the German armies crossed the Marne, again success petered out. On June 1st a German attack was met and repulsed by Americans. The Allies began to counter-attack. On August 8th a force of British, Canadians and Australians supported by 604 tanks (for the first time used *en masse*) went into action near Amiens. The German Army experienced its 'black day', on which it suffered 26,000 casualties. Having given everything left of their energy in an all-out bid for victory, the German troops were faced by an enemy beginning to counter-attack and refreshed by the arrival of vigorous, self-confident American reinforcements. Morale collapsed. By September the Allies were piercing the Hindenburg Line. This had previously been regarded as impregnable and represented the main German hope of maintaining a defensive position. Worse still, the German allies began to surrender, the Bulgarians in September, the Turks in October, the Austrians in November.

Dreams of triumph had been transformed into the nightmare of defeat.

3

The Weimar
Experiment

On March 22nd 1918 the Kaiser presented Hindenburg with the Iron Cross with Golden Rays in recognition of victory. On August 14th, Ludendorff informed the Kaiser, 'Germany can no longer hope to break the martial will of our enemies by military action.' Even the leaders were stunned and bewildered by the suddenness with which dreams of victory had been shattered.

Armistice negotiations did not begin until September 29th. On September 30th, Prince Max of Baden was asked to head a government and implement parliamentary monarchy. He took office hoping to arrange an honourable peace, but he was faced with the need to negotiate abject surrender. President Wilson of the United States made it increasingly clear that peace for him meant the dismissal of irresponsible princes. Military defeat was made worse by an increasingly effective British naval blockade. The Navy mutinied, widespread strikes broke out and rioting disturbed the capital. Fear arose that the Bolshevik catastrophe of Russia would be repeated in Germany. On November 9th Prince Max announced the Kaiser's abdication and appointed Friedrich Ebert, Chairman of the Social Democrat Party, as Chancellor.

Ludendorff had done his utmost to make a difficult situation impossible. When it became clear that Germany was to be treated as a defeated nation, he began to argue in favour of a last fight for survival. It was made plain that the civil authorities would not consider this and he was dismissed on October 26th. Not content with failure and inconsistency, he began to spread a poisonous myth to excuse defeat. Addressing the High Command, he declared, 'Let them now bear the consequences of what they have done to us.' The idea was put forward that the military forces had been betrayed at home. General Schulenburg on November 9th pronounced, 'Our men will claim that they were stabbed in the back by their comrades in arms, the Navy, together with Jewish war profiteers and shirkers.' Hindenburg also added his authority to this perverse lie.

Fortunately Ludendorff's successor, General Groener, had decided to promise Ebert the support of the Army in maintaining law and order, and Ebert set about forming a government. He was determined to resist pressure from the extreme Left, and he based his efforts on support from the moderate Socialists. Reforms were immediately begun to realise their ambitions. The 'Eight Hour Day' was introduced throughout Germany. Unemployment benefits were established. Demobilised troops were promised a return to work. Wage agreements between trade unions and employers were to be legally binding. All future elections would be based on universal suffrage for those over twenty years of age. National elections were indeed held on January 9th 1919. The Majority Social Democrats emerged as the largest party with 163 seats.

It is tempting to see the Social Democrat victory of 1919 as a natural Socialist victory after the collapse of the ruling classes of the Empire. This is however to exaggerate the change that occurred as a result of the 'November Revolution'. Ebert's co-operation with Prince Max and General Groener was regarded as a betrayal by the extreme Left. Led by Karl Liebknecht and Rosa Luxembourg, those Social Democrats who looked for a revolution on the Russian pattern formed a splinter group, first known as the Spartacists. On December 30th 1918 Liebknecht announced the formation of the German Communist Party. The Communists began to organise demonstrations. Ebert and the Minister of Defence, Gustav Noske, decided to crush these disorders. Units of *Freikorps*, demobilised adventurers anxious to retain an excuse for fighting, were let loose. Liebknecht and Luxembourg were hunted down and beaten to death. The Republic asserted its authority with Army approval by brutal and bloody force.

Furthermore, when the Weimar Republic began its work it was cruelly handicapped by association with the Treaty of Versailles signed in June 1919. The Allies decided to saddle Germany with responsibility for the war. The course of German expansion was reversed. Alsace and Lorraine were ceded to France, Eupen and Malmédy to Belgium. A plebiscite would decide the Danish-German frontier in Sleswig and the Polish-German frontier in Upper Silesia. Memel was given as a port to Lithuania. Worse still, German soil was handed over to the Czechs. The colonies, symbol of 'world power', were to be shared by the Allies. Perhaps these losses might have been expected, but the French were determined to ensure that Germany would never again menace her livelihood. The German Army was to be restricted to 100,000 men and have no tanks, heavy guns or aircraft. The Navy was restricted to six 10,000 ton battleships and no U-boats. Combined with loss of territory and limitation of arms was to be prolonged economic punishment. The Rhineland would be subject to Allied occupation for fifteen years. The Saar coal output was to go to France for the same period under Allied supervision. If these terms were harsh, the clause dealing with financial reparation was crippling. Germany was to repay to the Allies £6,600 million in gold. The combination of war guilt and excessive reparations, which can only perhaps be excused by remembering the treatment of the French in 1871, led to the widespread feeling that the Republic had betrayed Germany. Non-payment of reparations was referred to as a patriotic duty.

Nurtured in 'Red' blood, weighed down by the Treaty, the Republican Government nevertheless devised a theoretically democratic constitution. The Reich President was to be elected by the whole nation. He was to appoint the Chancellor and Reich Ministers, but disapproval by the Reichstag could lead to resignation or new elections. Although the federal states were still left with control of local government, the unity of the nation under government from Berlin was stressed. Universal suffrage, equality before the law, protection of private property, freedom of assembly and to petition were all stated to be 'basic rights and duties of Germans'. The underlying belief of the constitution was that all Germans agreed on basic principles. The events from 1919 to 1923 were to show that this belief was wildly optimistic.

The supporters of the Republican Government were faced with the depressing realities of political life in the German Reich. Although the rulers of the Kaiser's Empire had been discredited by failure, they remained as the political class with administrative experience. There might be a new

Freikorps members still displayed their military uniforms

political system, there was no new society. The Republicans had to rely on the bureaucrats, judges, professors, clergy, industrial magnates and General Staff that remained to direct the machinery of state. Many regarded the Republic as a temporary setback to be endured but not prolonged. Furthermore, with the growth of inflation the gap widened between the clever and powerful rich and the increasingly impoverished nation. While huge cartels spread and prospered, civil servants, clerks, wage-earners and pensioners were forced to spend their last remaining savings.

Most serious of all was the position of the Army. Before 1914, its members had been the *élite*, the gods and demigods of society. They were now in theory at least reduced to 100,000 men. Their new head, General von Seeckt, was anxious to maintain military tradition and gave the Republic grudging support. The demobilised soldiers were in many cases simply reformed into *Freikorps*, unofficial semi-military organisations violently nationalistic and spoiling for a showdown with the 'Bolshevik menace'. From the beginning the *Freikorps* introduced an ugly element into politics. They set out to intimidate the Poles of Upper Silesia and fought them in frequent street

27

battles. They then hounded the Communists in Berlin, and let loose a 'White Terror' against left wing elements in the Ruhr, Saxony and Thuringia.

In the first elections under the Weimar constitution the vote for the Social Democrats sagged and their representation was reduced to 102. The right wing elements attempted a *coup* in March 1920. The *Freikorps* had whetted their appetites on the Soldiers' and Workers' Councils. They now turned to the capture of Berlin. The Government fled. Significantly the *coup* failed not because the Government found enough military support to crush it but because a general strike paralysed its efforts. Von Seeckt remained malevolently neutral, and the *Freikorps* were not punished. Many of them took refuge in Bavaria where the infamous Captain Ehrhardt organised his Ehrhardt Brigade in planning assassination. In 1921 they struck down the leader of the Centre Party, Erzberger, who had signed the Versailles Treaty. In 1922 Rathenau, the Jewish Foreign Secretary, was also gunned down. His funeral was organised by the Government as a demonstration against right wing violence. This was temporarily effective but Republican order relied on very flimsy support. In Bavaria another right wing *coup* had succeeded, and Munich became the headquarters of right wing opposition to the Republic. Among several nationalist organisations there emerged the National Socialist Party. In July 1921 it elected as leader a certain Adolf Hitler, a name as yet unknown outside Bavaria.

Hitler was born in 1889 at Braunau just to the Austrian side of the border with Bavaria. His father had risen from cobbler's apprentice to customs official under the Habsburgs. The pension that went with this post enabled him to send Adolf to primary and secondary school. However, his son left school at sixteen with a poor academic record. He was rejected by the Academy of Fine Arts in Vienna. From 1908 to 1913 he lived as an 'art student' in Vienna. He earned a little money by selling paintings of views through the efforts of a Bohemian tramp. He read widely and developed violent phobias against priests, Habsburgs, Social Democrats and above all Jews. In the Austrian Empire the Jews dominated business and the professions. Embittered by failure, Hitler came increasingly to blame the Jews for his own lack of success as well as for policies he detested, like the granting of independence to nationalities under Habsburg rule. He warmly approved of Karl Lueger, Burgomaster of Vienna and ruthless anti-Semite.

In 1913 Hitler moved to Munich. He continued an aimless existence, frequenting cafés and beer cellars, always anxious to arouse unwilling listeners to the plight of Germans in Austria. He was delighted by the

29

◄ An official Nazi artist's version of an early German Workers' Party meeting arrival of war. 'I sank down on my knees and thanked Heaven,' he later wrote. He served as a runner at the Front. He was wounded twice and gassed. He rose to the rank of lance-corporal and received the Iron Cross, First Class, a decoration which was very uncommon among lance-corporals. He was noted for his quick temper and refusal to damn the war. While recovering from his wounds, Hitler was depressed by the morale of the people in Berlin and Munich. He attributed much of this to the Jews. 'Government offices were staffed by Jews. In the business world Jews had become indispensable. Like leeches they were slowly sucking the blood from the pores of the national body.' He was pleased to return to the Front and began to fear the treachery of politicians. He was gassed in the British attack on Ypres in 1918. While in hospital at Pasewalk in Pomerania, he heard the news of defeat from the local pastor. Hitler broke down and wept.

When demobilised, Hitler returned to Munich. He lived through violent political changes there, and became a Political Instruction Officer for the Munich District Military Command. He met and made friends with Major Roehm, a *Freikorps* leader. In September 1919 he was sent to investigate a meeting of the German Workers' Party. He found a meeting of not more than twenty-five people in a beer cellar. He made a violently nationalist speech and was invited to join the committee of six. Party funds consisted of 7.5 marks. Hitler at once concentrated on publicity, improving posters and advertising in the press. His methods brought success. At Hitler's first meeting in October 1919, 111 people attended. By February 1920 his audience was 2,000. Major Roehm directed *Freikorps* members into the Party, and he also helped to organise strong-arm squads aiming to be at least as tough as the Communists. Most important of all, Roehm persuaded his superior, Major-General Epp, to raise the capital of 60,000 marks to finance a newspaper.

Hitler's importance in the Party gradually grew. When the Party changed its name to the National Socialist Workers' Party, Hitler quarrelled with its founder Drexler over the relative importance of the 'National' and 'Socialist' elements. By July 1921 he had outmanoeuvred Drexler and become President of the Party. The early development of the Party un-doubtedly owed much to Hitler's personal talents. He grasped the vital importance of propaganda, particularly the news value of violence. He gradually mastered the technique of hammering home a simple explosive message into the minds of a lower middle-class audience. It is interesting to note that he admired the English Prime Minister Lloyd George's skill in this respect. He carefully designed a dramatic banner. The red background infuriated the Communists, the black swastika pleased the nationalists. Above all he developed the regimented strong-arm men that from October 1921 were to be known as the *Sturmabteilung* or Storm Section (SA). He taught them the simple lesson that 'force replaced sense'.

By October 1922 he was sufficiently confident to take eight hundred Stormtroopers to Coburg to parade and fight a pitched battle with the extreme Left in spite of a police ban. However, Hitler himself admitted that success would depend on the weakness or strength of Republican government. Events were soon to test whether this was true.

4

Reparations, Revival, Slump

The revulsion of feeling caused by the murder of Walter Rathenau, the Foreign Minister, encouraged the Berlin Government to take decisive action against terrorism. They passed the Law for the Protection of the Republic. Heavy penalties were threatened for political violence. The weakness of the Government's authority was indicated when the Bavarian authorities issued an emergency decree suspending this law in Bavaria. Although the Berlin Government succeeded in getting this withdrawn, the result was a further move to the right in Bavaria. However, although the challenge from Bavaria was serious, the Berlin Government was faced with worse problems elsewhere.

In 1918 the German mark was valued at four to the dollar. By the summer of 1922 it had reached four hundred to the dollar. The Government informed the Allied Powers that it could not maintain payment of reparations. Unhappily for Germany, France reacted by giving power to Raymond Poincaré who in January 1922 became both Prime and Foreign Minister. Poincaré had witnessed the German occupation of France in 1870, and he combined fierce nationalism with the rigidly legalistic mind of a trained lawyer. He decided that Germany must be made to pay for her failure to keep up payment. His distrust was heightened by the fact that Germany had opened relations with Soviet Russia in April 1922. He also deplored the failure of the German Government to halt inflation or prevent rich industrialists from speculating with the mark.

On January 11th 1923 French and Belgian troops occupied the Ruhr. 'We are going to look for coal, that is all,' Poincaré declared. Germany united in fury. The Government declared a policy of non-co-operation and passive resistance. *Saboteurs* blew up bridges and derailed trains. The French retaliated with arrests and deportations. The paralysis of the Ruhr, which accounted for eighty per cent of Germany's coal, steel and pig iron, completed the collapse of the mark. By July 1st 1923 it was worth 160,000 to the dollar, on November 1st 130,000,000,000. The occupation of the Ruhr had totally destroyed the value of the money with which reparations might be paid.

In August 1923 Gustav Stresemann, leader of the German People's Party, formed a government to stabilise the economy. The French were forced to accept a panel of economic experts led by the American Dawes. The Dawes Plan recommended French evacuation of the Ruhr and the reinflation of the German economy backed by a huge international loan. Frenchmen recognised Poincaré's failure and voted him from office in May 1924.

The collapse of the mark presented Hitler with a great opportunity. In 1922 he served a short prison sentence for organising violence. On his release after only five weeks his denunciations of the Berlin Government as the 'November Criminals' reached a new pitch of hysteria and hatred. The collapse of the mark, added to such humiliations as the League of Nations intervening in Upper Silesia to enlarge Polish territory at German expense, seemed to justify Hitler's most extreme claims. All classes of society except the richest industrialists and landowners were faced with misery and despair. The Communists rose in rebellion in October 1923, and Independent Socialists in Saxony and Thuringia threatened to set up separatist states. The 'Bolshevik menace' seemed to be materialising. Hitler and Roehm organised the banding together of Bavarian patriotic leagues in the Fighting Association. The crisis came to boiling point on September 16th 1923 when Stresemann, acting with the support of the Social Democrats, announced the end of passive resistance in the Ruhr and the renewal of reparations.

Hitler and his allies organised massive demonstrations. Their confidence was increased by the Bavarian government's reaction to Stresemann's policy. Von Kahr, a noted reactionary, was granted dictatorial powers, and

Flanked by Ludendorff and Roehm at the time of
their trial after the Munich *Putsch*, Hitler makes
the most of his new-found prominence

the Bavarian army swore an oath of allegiance to him. Most important of all,
the new Bavarian Minister of Justice was Franz Gürtner who was sympathetic to Hitler.

However, the role of the Army in this crisis was to prove crucial. The
German High Command under von Seeckt came to the aid of Stresemann
and crushed the Communist and Socialist risings with enthusiasm. The
Bavarian government took fright. An attempt by Hitler to let loose 20,000
Stormtroopers on the Socialists celebrating May Day had been frustrated
by the forcible disarming of the SA by the regular troops. Significantly,
Hitler escaped prosecution through the good offices of the Minister of
Justice. After this fiasco he recovered prestige sufficiently to attend and

address a massive rally of patriotic associations on September 2nd 1923 to commemorate the victory of Sedan in 1870. He stood by the side of Ludendorff. Dramatic action became essential, just as the Bavarian government began to urge caution.

Hitler decided on a sudden revolutionary move or *putsch* on the night of November 8th. He was anxious that his leadership would not be overshadowed by some action of the Bavarian government. Von Kahr, General Lossow, the Bavarian Commander, and other political leaders were due to address a packed rally in a beer cellar. Hitler surrounded the hall with six hundred SA, and stationed a machine-gun in the entrance. After firing a pistol in the air, he announced, 'The National Revolution has begun.' The politicians were bluffed into pledging support. Ludendorff was summoned to join them. The meeting broke up amid cheering and intense excitement.

However, during the night Hitler failed to seize control of either the Munich garrison or police headquarters. The senior army officers decided to crush the *putsch*, and Kahr and Lossow dissociated themselves from it. Hitler feared failure, Ludendorff urged action. Next morning, at the head of two to three thousand supporters, Ludendorff and Hitler marched on the War Ministry to join Roehm. Although outnumbered by thirty to one, the police fired carbines at the leaders as they marched down the Residenzstrasse. In a minute sixteen National Socialists were dead. Ludendorff continued marching. No one followed him. Hitler, who had been linked with the arm of one of the dead, was the first to flee in a yellow motor car. Two days later he was arrested at Uffing.

The ease with which the Munich *putsch* was dispersed might well have meant the end of a less extraordinary man than Hitler. Instead he turned his trial into a triumph of propaganda. Owing to the prominence of the accused and accusers—Ludendorff, Kahr, Lossow—the trial was headline news for twenty-four days. Hitler revelled in exaggerated responsibility for the crimes for which he was accused. 'I alone bear the responsibility.' 'One day the hour will come when the Reichswehr (the German Army) will stand at our side.' 'Judgement is spoken by the eternal court of history.' Protected by a judicial tolerance contrived once again by the Minister of Justice, Hitler made himself into a figure of national note. His sentence was the minimum possible, five years. In fact he stayed at Landsberg prison in comfortable conditions for just over a year.

However, by the time Hitler was released on December 20th 1924, Stresemann's government had weathered its crisis. Dr Schlacht had been appointed President of the Reichsbank to stabilise the economy. A new Rentenmark was established equal to one billion old marks. By the summer of 1924 confidence was restored. Germany was built up again largely due to the desire of the Allies to revive normal international, political and financial relations. The Dawes Plan removed the occupying forces from the Ruhr, and in October 1925 the Locarno Pact guaranteed the mutual frontiers of France, Germany and Belgium. In 1926 Germany was formally reconciled with the Soviet Union and invited to join the League of Nations, the international assembly, by a unanimous vote. In 1928 Stresemann joined the Kellogg–Briand Pact organised by France and America to renounce war. Very large investments, particularly from America, re-inflated the economy. Loans of thirty thousand million marks ensured the payment of reparations as well as the amenity of social services.

German industrial production doubled in four years. Real wages rose by ten per cent. Unemployment fell to 650,000 by the summer of 1928. Furthermore, culture returned to a Germany revived by the growing sense of social stability. Thomas Mann produced a great novel, *Magic Mountain*, Brecht the startling *Threepenny Opera*. The Bauhaus architectural experiments and Kurt Hahn's educational ideas were talking points for the intellectuals of Europe.

The success of the Republican Government was reflected in election results. In May 1924 the extremists prospered. The Communists obtained sixty-two Reichstag seats, the National Socialists (Nazis) thirty-two seats. By 1928 the Nazis had slumped to twelve seats. Nevertheless, although the Social Democrats increased their representation from one hundred to one hundred and fifty-three seats, they never regained the strength of 1919. Furthermore, when President Ebert died in 1925, Germany replaced him with a symbol of their past, the conservative monarchist, Field Marshal Hindenburg, who was backed by the Nazis among others.

Hitler's stay in prison, from November 11th 1923 to December 20th 1924, gave several insights into his methods and future problems. He largely busied himself with writing a long, repetitive and rambling account of his career in the book *Mein Kampf* (My Struggle). This provides interest mainly because of its record of Hitler's ideas and fears.

Hitler's overriding obsession in the book is the need for the German nation to preserve its purity in descent from the Aryans, 'the founders of culture', who originated in Central Asia. He sees this purity threatened by corruption from the Jews. His hatred of the Jews is hysterical and vicious. In

Hitler at Landsberg Prison

one passage he argues that, 'On putting the probing knife to any form of foulness, especially in cultural life, one immediately discovers, like a maggot in a putrescent body, a little Jew who is often blinded by the sudden light.' Jewish control of the press, cinema and theatre is compared with the 'black plague of long ago.' Hitler regarded the prime quality of the Aryan to be the possession of a strength of will which achieves mastery in life's natural struggle. He sees this as involving for Germany 'settling with France' and achievement of living space in the East at the expense of 'degenerate Slavs.' The best summary of his view of life comes in the sentence, 'The whole organisation of education and training, which the People's State must take as its crowning task, is the work of instilling into the hearts and brains of the youth entrusted to it, the racial instinct and understanding of the racial idea.' The most remarkable ingredient of *Mein Kampf* is the section explaining the vital political role of propaganda. This is

37

almost the only passage in the book that revealed Hitler's potential as a practical politician of genius.

While devoting himself to the task of achieving what he hoped would be intellectual distinction, Hitler seemed content to allow the Nazi Party to disintegrate and flounder. He deliberately appointed the second-rate Rosenberg as his deputy. This tidy-minded intellectual soon found himself at odds with the violent Jew baiters. Moreover splits widened between the Protestant, middle-class northerners and the more radical, Catholic Bavarians. Hitler was content to witness divisions which failed to threaten his personal leadership. His main concern in this respect was the growing success of Roehm in building up a private army of some 30,000 militarists.

When Hitler was released, the Nazi representation in the Reichstag had sunk to fourteen in the second elections of 1924. In January 1925 the Minister President of Bavaria lifted the ban on the Party and its paper which had been imposed after the Munich *Putsch*. He explained his action with, 'The wild beast is checked. We can afford to loosen the chain.'

That Hitler was a force to reckon with soon became obvious. On February 24th 1925 he brought wild cheers from a crowd of 4,000 by attacking Marxism and Jewry. He was banned from further speeches and meetings in Bavaria until May 1927. This ban was repeated in several other states. Perhaps it was this that led to Hitler's decision to seek future success in election rather than from revolution. He retired to a villa above Berchtesgaden in the Bavarian Alps. He seems to have lived on the proceeds of writing and Party dues, as well as donations from the sympathetic Duchess of Sachsen-Anhalt. He left most of the Party work to Gregor Strasser and a new recruit, an educated Rhinelander, Paul Josef Goebbels. Strasser tried to accentuate the Socialist ingredient in Nazi policy and actually persuaded Goebbels to propose Hitler's expulsion from the Party for refusing to co-operate. Hitler, however, faced Strasser and Goebbels and succeeded in winning Goebbels over as a lasting convert.

The growing stability of the Republican regime gave Hitler the chance to develop the Party without arousing alarm. In July 1926 Hitler for the first time used his stiff arm salute at a rally in Nuremberg, one of the few cities in which he was not banned. In November Goebbels was given the title of Gauleiter of Berlin. As a paid party official he was to promote Hitler's interest at the expense of Strasser and his brother. One of the survivors of Munich, Hermann Goering, an ex-air ace, returned in 1927 and was encouraged to cultivate respectable support. In 1929 a chicken farmer,

Heinrich Himmler, began to build up the *Schutz Staffeln* (SS or Select Guard), a black-shirted rival force to the SA, sworn to be Hitler's personal bodyguard. The Party began to develop subsections for different affairs, including Propaganda and the Hitler Youth. Membership rose steadily from 17,000 in 1926 to 60,000 by the end of 1928.

1929 was to prove a decisive year for Hitler. An international committee of economic experts led by the American banker Owen D. Young decided that Germany could reduce her reparations payment but must continue to pay for fifty-nine years. Stresemann managed to link this Young Plan with the withdrawal of occupying forces from the Rhineland. Right wing forces united in denouncing reparations as a national humiliation. Alfred Hugenberg, ex-Krupp director, newspaper owner and supported by the largest ex-servicemen's organisation, chose Hitler as his mouthpiece. Hugenberg and Hitler attempted to pass 'A Law against the Enslavement of the German People.' It failed, but until March 1930 Hitler exploited the publicity of Hugenberg's national chain of newspapers. His skill as an inflammatory orator was noticed by rich businessmen like the Ruhr industrialist Emil Kindorf. Hitler cleverly blamed Hugenberg's comparative moderation for the failure of the campaign to prevent the passing of the Young Plan. He was now a national figure. Party membership spiralled from 120,000 in August 1929 to 210,000 in March 1930.

Just as he achieved status as a national politician, the disaster which he had so energetically prophesied materialised. On October 3rd 1929, Stresemann died, worn out by bolstering up the Republic. Three weeks later the New York stock market underwent a sensational collapse. The economic backbone of Germany crumbled into dust.

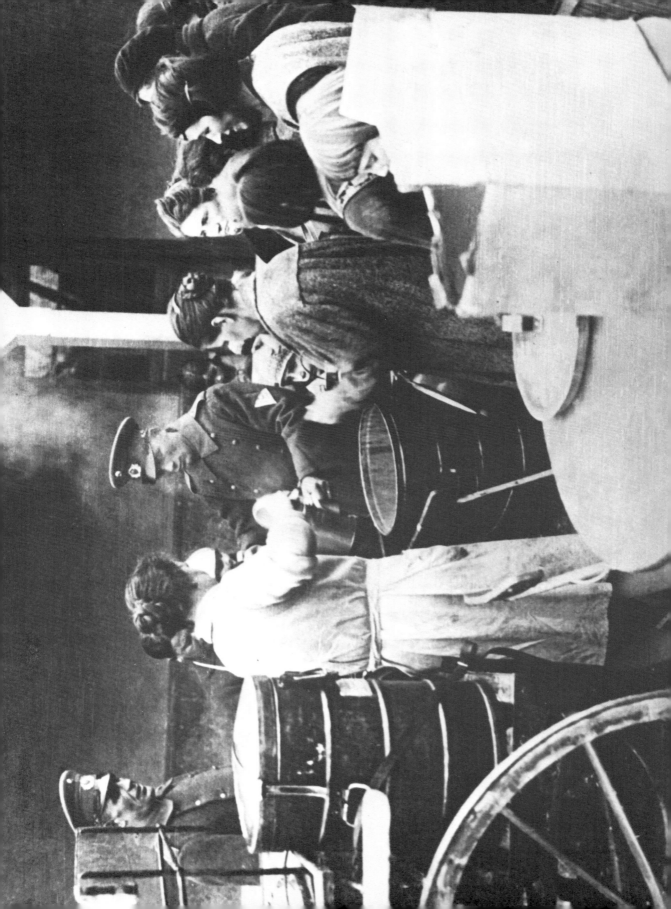

5

The Nazis come
to Power

The depression which began in the United States in 1929 and hit Germany with full force in 1931 was a demoralising phenomenon. The most advanced capitalist economies of the West, riding high on a wave of industrial expansion and feverish investment, suddenly collapsed. The thoughtless optimism which had inflated the boom of the late nineteen-twenties gave way to mindless despair. The collapse of credit struck hard at many levels of society. Banks and factories closed. Thousands of small businesses went bankrupt. Ripe harvests rotted in the fields through lack of buyers. For the workers, the queue for unemployment benefits and the increasingly forlorn hope of work became a depressing daily experience. The middle classes saw hard-gained property and respectability snatched from their grasp.

In Germany the loss was particularly bitter. The memories of defeat in 1918 and inflation in 1923 were just becoming comfortingly distant when disaster returned. The dependence on foreign investment was disastrous to industry. The agricultural income for 1932–3 was a billion marks below the previous worst year since the war. Workers, tradesmen, newly-trained graduates and professional classes alike joined the ever-increasing ranks of the unemployed: 1,320,000 in September 1929, 3,000,000 a year later, 4,350,000 by 1931 and even passing the 6,000,000 mark by February 1933. Only the richest businessmen and landowners could still enjoy prosperity.

◀ Army soup kitchens provide food for German unemployed, 1931

The rest were gripped by hatred for 'the System' which had betrayed them.

The tragedy for Germany was that the Weimar experiment had not produced a form of government capable of dealing with anything like such a serious crisis. The last Social Democrat Chancellor, Hermann Mueller, was forced to resign in March 1930. The coalition of democratic parties split into quarrelling factions over the decision to impose higher contributions to pay for the unemployment fund. The democratic failure was demonstrated by the fact that the new Chancellor, Heinrich Bruening, was manoeuvred into power by the latest in the line of political generals, Kurt von Schleicher.

Schleicher was an obsessive intriguer of considerable skill, who succeeded in gaining the ear of the President's son, Oskar von Hindenburg. He was determined to exploit the most vulnerable point of the Weimar constitution, Article 48. This gave the President power to rule by emergency decree in times of crisis. Schleicher intended that the sober, conservative Bruening, leader of the respectable Catholic Centre, would be the tool of the Army and the forces of reaction in the use of the decree. However, while the small group round the President manoeuvred for position, Hitler was busy converting national disillusionment into National Socialist votes.

The depression presented Hitler with his outstanding opportunity. In 1928 the Nazis commanded only twelve Reichstag seats: by September 1930 they had become the second largest party in Germany. The fact that Hitler had played so little part in the previous government proved to be an advantage. He was unembarrassed by the failure of 'the System'. He alone had persistently forecast disaster. He was acutely aware of the opportunity which was presented to him. He wrote, 'Never in my life have I been so well disposed and inwardly contented as in these days.'

The crucial opportunity arose on July 16th 1930, when Bruening's measures to cope with the economic crisis were rejected by the Reichstag. Bruening decided to call an election. Hitler and Goebbels reacted vigorously. The Nazi campaign was exceptionally thorough. An agricultural expert, Walther Darré, produced a programme directed at the peasant vote. Hitler and Goebbels spoke unceasingly, denouncing politicians, economists and above all 'Jewish' war profiteers for 'debasing the will of Germany'. The result surprised even Hitler. The Nazis polled 6,409,000 votes and captured 107 seats. Significantly, the only other party to make an impressive gain was the Communist Party with an increase from 54 to 77 seats. Ten other parties polled more than a million votes. No workable coalition seemed likely. The Nazis and Communists were united only by their hostility to the Republic.

Hitler delighted in his newly-acquired prominence. Foreign correspondents were lectured on the role of the Nazis as a bulwark against Bolshevism. Many were impressed. Hitler did not however remain idle. He began his campaign to make sure that, 'Democracy must be defeated with the weapons of democracy.' He realised the essential need for support from the Army and big industrialists. His handling of intrigue was extraordinarily complex and successfully overcame apparently decisive setbacks.

Much of the most vigorous support for the Nazis came from the SA. This riotous and violent body, now more than four times the size of the Army, aroused fear and horror among the professional officer class. Hitler managed to make full use of street battles against the Communists as propaganda. One of his favourite sayings was, 'Possession of the streets is the key to the power in the State.' At the same time, a special issue of the Party paper, the *Völkischer Beobachter* (People's Observer), was printed for the Army. Hitler spoke at great length at the trial of three lieutenants at Leipzig, emphasising his regard for the Army and the non-revolutionary nature of the SA. A fine distinction was drawn between the degree of violence necessary to intimidate Nazi opponents and the 'excessive' use, which could be interpreted as aiming at a *putsch*.

Similarly Hitler began to court industrialists to provide the money essential to the Nazi propaganda machine. A powerful group of coal and steel producers, notably Emil Kindorf and Fritz Thyssen, began to subscribe substantial amounts to Party funds. A meeting was arranged in Goering's flat in January 1931 with Dr Schacht. The decisive triumph occurred in January 1932 at a meeting arranged by Fritz Thyssen of the Industrial Club at the Park Hotel, Düsseldorf. Hitler developed at length his main argument, 'The Power State creates for the business world the general conditions for its subsequent prosperity.' The industrialists rose and cheered Hitler. They went on to provide decisive financial support.

At the same time as he got the backing of the wealthy and powerful few, Hitler was also aware that his strength lay in the size of the popular vote. The Strasser brothers continually urged a more radical approach. Hitler's attitude was characteristic; he used radical gestures to win support and increase the fear he inspired with the right wing, but, when forced to choose, always came down on the side of big money and established order. His true views were expressed to Otto Strasser. 'The great mass of working men

43

want only bread and circuses. They have no understanding for ideals of any sort whatsoever.'

The year 1931 witnessed the failure of Bruening to cope with the economic crisis. He tried the classic remedies of deflation, extra taxes, cuts in salaries and wages and unemployment benefits. These measures were naturally extremely unpopular and they did not work. Furthermore Bruening's prestige was undermined by the success of the French in wrecking his projected customs union with Austria. General Schleicher began to withdraw his confidence from Bruening and devise schemes for making use of the Nazis. However, Hitler failed to impress either Bruening or Hindenburg. The old President seems to have assessed him as a possible Minister of Posts. The deepening economic crisis made the winter of 1931 particularly dismal. Government restrictions and the number of unemployed increased together. Nazi Party membership doubled to around 800,000. Nazis did well in state elections. Hitler kept up his attack on Bruening whom he pictured as the embodiment of the evils of 'the System'. On January 6th 1932, Bruening publicly recognised the importance of Hitler by bringing him into discussions on the coming Presidential elections.

The announcement of new Presidential elections placed Hitler in a dilemma. Should he oppose Hindenburg and risk defeat or not intervene and miss the chance of establishing himself as his likely successor? After considerable debate and hesitation, on February 22nd he allowed Goebbels to announce his candidature at the Berlin Sports Palace to a wildly cheering crowd. Significantly this was a week after he had obtained the backing of the Industrial Club. Hitler and Goebbels repaid investment by political talent of a high order. After Hitler had been hurriedly registered as a German citizen by the Nazi regime of Brunswick, the campaign began in earnest. Canvassing was carried out with meticulous thoroughness. All the mechanics of modern advertising were employed, posters, films and gramophone records. Hitler and Goebbels introduced the techniques now regarded as essential. Above all, they made almost incessant speeches. The result was a vote for Hitler of 11,500,000, for Hindenburg of 18,662,000. Hitler had not won, but he had prevented Hindenburg getting an overall majority, and another election became necessary. Hitler rebounded with enthusiasm. 'The first election campaign is over. The second has begun today. I shall lead it.'

Campaigning reached a new fever pitch. Hitler took to using an aeroplane. His arrivals were stage-managed, making use of a searchlight and

Hitler and Roehm at an early Party meeting at Brunswick

often defying very bad weather conditions. He spoke in twenty-six towns in nine days. He increased his vote by two million. However, Hindenburg's vote went up by one million to give him a crucial fifty-three per cent. He appeared to have survived the threat from Hitler on the Right and also from the Communist candidate on the Left, who polled ten per cent.

The problem of how to deal with the Nazis remained. Bruening and the Minister of Defence, General Groener, were increasingly alarmed by the violence of the Nazi supporters. The Hesse authorities revealed the discovery of plans for a take-over by the SA in the event of a Communist uprising. Three days after the Presidential election, Bruening and Groener ordered the banning of the SS and the SA, now 400,000 strong. They merely ceased wearing uniforms. Their organisation remained defiantly intact.

45

Bruening and Groener were being edged out of power by the further intrigues of General Schleicher. On the 30th, Bruening resigned at Hindenburg's request, and Hindenburg instructed Franz von Papen to form a government above parties. Von Papen charmed Hindenburg. Descended from Westphalian nobility, a wealthy industrialist by marriage, he had smooth and courtly manners. Unfortunately, he completely lacked political backing and was even expelled by his own political party, the Centre, which remained loyal to Bruening. Von Papen formed a cabinet of right wing nobility, two managing directors and Gürtner, Bavarian Minister and old protector of Hitler. He dissolved the Reichstag and on June 16th lifted the ban on the SA and SS.

The Nazis switched on their full electoral power. The political campaign became frighteningly violent. On July 10th, the Nazis and the 'Reds' fought a battle in the streets of Altona, involving nineteen dead and two hundred and eighty-five wounded. Von Papen responded by banning political parades and deposing the Prussian government for failing to maintain order. The Socialist ministers were removed by armed troops. Von Papen was declared Reich Commissioner for Prussia. When the election results were announced, the Nazis had 13,745,000 votes and 230 seats, the Social Democrats had 133 seats, the Communists 89, the Centre 73, Hugenberg's National Party, which alone had supported von Papen, a derisory 44 seats. Hitler was now the leader of overwhelmingly the most powerful party in Germany.

After his success in the election of July 31st, Hitler expected to gain the Chancellorship for himself, control of Prussia for the Party and a new post for Goebbels in charge of 'Popular Enlightenment and Propaganda'. Hitler thought he had won over Schleicher, but Schleicher and von Papen left the decision to Hindenburg. The President in his eighty-fifth year interviewed Hitler standing up and gave him a lecture on the need to discipline the violence of his party and to command a majority in the Reichstag. Hitler was out-manoeuvred and faced with the restive SA anxious for revolution.

Hitler seems to have decided to adopt an increasingly radical and more openly violent line. He publicly supported five SA men who had kicked to death a Communist miner in front of his mother at Potempa. The Nazis combined with the Centre Party to elect Goering President of the Reichstag. Goering engineered a vote of censure on von Papen's government by a vote of 513 to 32, and von Papen was compelled once more to call for new elections on November 6th.

By this time the country was becoming tired of election fever. The Nazis were running out of money and Hitler's industrialist backers were alarmed by his radical line and his support for a transport strike in Berlin. However, although the Nazi vote fell by two million, with one hundred and ninety-six seats they were still decidedly the largest party in the Reichstag.

Schleicher and von Papen intrigued each other out of power in vain attempts to convince Hindenburg of their capacity to command a Reichstag majority. Each failed in the attempt. Hitler, sensing that his opportunity was near, blamed Gregor Strasser for the radicalism the Nazis had displayed. Finance again became available, and a group of industrialists and bankers urged Hindenburg to let Hitler form a cabinet. Hitler won the support of Oskar von Hindenburg. Finally von Papen devised a scheme by which Hitler became Chancellor, another Nazi, Frick, Minister of the Interior and Goering Minister of the Interior for Prussia. Von Papen was Vice-Chancellor. Eight other ministries were to be held by the Conservatives. The Army supported the scheme. Von Papen was confident he could handle Hitler. Hindenburg was anxious to be rid of Schleicher.

At midday on January 30th, 1933, Hitler was sworn in as Chancellor. By nightfall the streets were filled with processions of torch-bearing cheering Nazis.

6

The Nazi Revolution

The first six months of 1933 revealed for the first time the full extent of Hitler's political genius. When he became Chancellor, there was some considerable likelihood that von Papen's schemes to make use of the Nazis in the interest of the parties of the Right might succeed. Hitler had never been backed by more than thirty-seven per cent of the electorate, and his vote was declining. Neither he nor his henchmen had any significant experience of government administration. He owed his appointment to von Papen's intrigues. Von Papen as Vice-Chancellor had established the right to be present at all meetings with the President, with whom he was confident of decisive influence. Above all von Papen was sure that with all his worldly experience he could outwit 'the Bohemian corporal', as the old guard liked to call Hitler. In fact it was Hitler who took the initiative and by a series of callous and unprincipled moves established a dictatorship.

Hitler displayed a capacity for decisive action of an exceptional and diabolical order. Within five hours of becoming Chancellor, he held his first cabinet meeting. He at once raised the question of the need to command a Reichstag majority and the impossibility of achieving this without the seventy seats held by the Centre. He suggested that unless he could get the co-operation of the Centre new elections were necessary. Hugenberg and von Papen reluctantly agreed. In practice Hitler rejected even discussion of

49

◄ Hitler with Roehm and Goering at the
height of the SA's power

the Centre's terms and announced that elections would take place on March 5th. Goebbels was delighted. 'Now it will be easy,' he wrote in his diary.

The full forces of the State were mobilised by the Nazis. Control of the radio was added to their previous instruments of propaganda. On February 20th Goering entertained the leaders of business in the Reichstag President's palace. Dr Schacht acted as host to about twenty-five of Germany's greatest financiers, including Krupp von Bohlen, directors of the great chemical combine I. G. Farben and the head of the United Steel Works. Goering boasted that they need not worry about a repetition of contributions towards election costs. 'March 5th will surely be the last election for ten years, probably even for one hundred years.' Hitler promised to smash Marxism and revive the Army. This opened tempting opportunities for manufacturers of chemicals and steel. Dr Schacht estimated the collection at three million marks.

At the same time government authority was employed to support a policy of intimidation. Communist meetings and publications were banned. Social Democrat rallies were either broken up or forbidden. Even Bruening had to seek police protection from SA thugs. In Prussia, which meant two-thirds of Germany, Goering used his ministerial position to bring the complete range of officials under Nazi control. He urged the police to use firearms against those 'hostile to the State'. To underline the point he recruited 50,000 auxiliary police of whom 40,000 were members of the SA or SS.

Rather surprisingly, the Communists were not provoked into an uprising, and it therefore became necessary to invent one. On the night of February 27th, the Reichstag building was found to be ablaze. The Berlin SA leader, Karl Ernst, had spread inflammable material, making use of a tunnel from Goering's palace. A Dutch Communist and simpleton, van der Lubbe, was allowed to set fire to the building. The next day Hindenburg signed a decree for 'The Protection of the People and the State'. Individual and civil liberties were overthrown in defence against 'Communist acts of violence'. Forty thousand Communist officials and many Social Democrat leaders were arrested in a Nazi Terror. Lorry loads of brown-shirted 'officials' paraded shouting and singing through the streets, smashing what they pleased. Goering summarised his approach with, 'Dear Communists, I shall lead the struggle to the death in which my fist will grasp your necks.' Only Bruening dared voice disapproval and he was ignored.

When the votes were counted on March 5th, the Nazis had captured 288 seats out of 647, but they still had only forty-four per cent of the vote. The tragedy was that there was no combination capable of resistance. The Social Democrats had no hope of combining with the Communists, whose policy was in fact to support the Nazis rather than the Republic. The National and Centre Parties were hopelessly compromised by their association with the Nazis. At all events, Hitler was about to demonstrate the fate of electoral decisions in his hands.

On March 21st, Goebbels organised one of the great theatrical events of German history. The new Reichstag was summoned to a ceremony at the Garrison Church in Potsdam. It was the shrine of the old order, the site of Frederick the Great's tomb. March 21st was the anniversary of Bismarck's opening of the first Reichstag of the Empire in 1871. All the Kaiser's surviving generals and even the Crown Prince were displayed in historic uniform. The exiled Kaiser's chair was left vacant. Hindenburg presided. Superimposed on the symbols of the past were the emblems of the present. Nazi swastikas dominated the scene.

Hitler made a dignified and carefully calculated speech, ending with the words, 'By a unique upheaval in the last few weeks our national honour has been restored and, thanks to your understanding, *Herr Generalfeldmarschall*, the union between the symbols of the old greatness and the new strength has been celebrated. We pay you our homage. A protective providence places you over the new forces of our nation.' Hitler then bowed low and gripped the President's hand.

Two days later when the Reichstag met at the Kroll Opera House in Berlin, the deputies found it surrounded by SS and lined with SA along the walls. A huge swastika flag covered one wall. They were introduced by Hitler to the Enabling Bill. The Government was to be given power for four years to enact laws without the Reichstag. This power included the right to alter the Constitution and sign treaties. Laws could be drafted by the Chancellor and become law the day after publication. Hitler made fulsome promises that the rights of the President, the Federal States and the Churches would not be undermined. He emphasised the expected rarity of the need to use the Bill.

Most of the deputies were mesmerised by the combination of the threat of force and expressions of legality. Outside the SS bayed promises of fire and blood. The Communists had been outlawed. Only the Social Democrat leader, Otto Wels, dared to oppose. Hitler raved, 'Your death knell has sounded.' The Bill was passed by 441 votes to 94. The result was greeted with cries of triumph and the singing of the *Horst Wessel Song*, a propagandist hymn in memory of a Nazi 'martyr'.

On May 1st 1933 Hitler repeated his tactic of preceding violence by splendid ceremony. May Day was celebrated on an unprecedented scale. 100,000 workers at the Tempelhof airfield were addressed by Hitler and recited his slogan, 'Honour work and respect the worker!' Early next day, the SA and SS occupied trade union headquarters throughout the country, confiscated funds and either arrested or beat up union leaders. All unions were merged into the German Labour Front. By the end of May collective bargaining by workers was banned by law.

Political parties and state assemblies suffered a similar fate. The Social Democrats were dissolved as 'subversive and hostile to the State'. The Centre and People's Parties and the Democrats resigned. Even Hitler's ally, the German National Party, was seized, smashed and 'voluntarily' dissolved. Hugenberg resigned from the government. On July 14th a law decreed, 'The Nazi Party constitutes the only political party in Germany.' Even before the passing of the Enabling Bill, the Nazis had carried out a *putsch* in Bavaria. Hitler, acting from memory no doubt, made sure the Army did not interfere. All state assemblies were dissolved on March 31st. State governors were appointed to regulate appointments of judges and government officials, even state orchestral players. They were to carry out policy laid down by the Chancellor. On January 30th 1934, a Law for the Reconstruction of the Reich abolished all 'popular assemblies'. State governments became purely administrative departments.

By the summer of 1933 Hitler had successfully crushed popular opposition outside the Nazi Party. The question now arose of how far the Nazi revolution would go. Roehm and Goebbels were in favour of launching 'a second revolution' against big business, the *Junker* landlords and above all the professional Army dominated by the Prussian generals. Hitler made it increasingly clear where he stood. Only three days after receiving office, he addressed the leading admirals and generals, promising them privately that they need not fear civil war and could devote their energies to expansion and rearmament. Hitler attached great significance to the role of General von Blomberg as Minister of Defence. On April 4th 1933 he set up the Reich Defence Council to plan rearmament. On July 20th he introduced an Army Law which restored the rights of the Officer Corps to be independent of civil courts. Roehm by contrast was anxious to form a national army based

Field Marshal von Mackensen, General Ludendorff, President Hindenburg
and General von Seeckt at the Tannenberg Memorial Parade, 1933. Behind
the President stands his son, Oskar von Hindenburg

on the SA, now over two million strong. He referred to the Prussian generals
as 'old clods'.

Many of the SA and Nazi rank and file had been drawn from the unemployed and underprivileged anxious to take over employers' associations
and smash large department stores. Hitler addressed the state governors
on July 6th and made his own position quite clear. 'In business, ability
must be the only standard.' He restored Krupp and Thyssen as leaders of
the Employers' Association and dissolved the Nazi Combat League

of Middleclass Tradesmen. Furthermore his appointment as Minister of Economics in place of Hugenberg was Dr Karl Schmitt, Director of Germany's largest insurance firm, Allianz. Although a clash with Roehm was inevitable, Hitler lulled him into a sense of security by publishing a letter of gratitude and praise to, 'My dear Ernst Roehm, for your imperishable services,' on January 1st 1934.

Hitler's personal position was demonstrated to be on a very firm popular basis by the end of 1934. His first intrusion into foreign affairs had been triumphantly endorsed. In May he promised the world enduring peace and the suspension of armaments provided that Germany received equality of treatment with other nations. On October 4th, he announced Germany's withdrawal from the Disarmament Conference at Geneva and the League of Nations because of the failure of the Great Powers to promise reduction of arms in under eight years. The Powers remained divided and inactive. Hitler evoked genuine delight in Germany as a leader who was prepared to assert an independent German line.

However, although the nation might applaud, the group of advisers around Hindenburg was less enthusiastic. Furthermore it became increasingly clear that the life of the President was coming to its close. Hitler saw that the support of the Army would be vital. Disturbing rumours came through to him that Hindenburg and some of the 'old guard' favoured a Hohenzollern restoration. On April 11th, Hitler took the initiative. Accompanied by the Commanders-in-Chief on the cruiser *Deutschland* on the way to spring manoeuvres, he proposed that he should be successor to Hindenburg and in return for Army support offered drastic curbing of the numbers and power of the SA. By May 16th, the agreement of the Navy and Army High Command had been achieved.

Himmler and Goering built up increasingly large personal forces to use against what they saw as a dangerous rival. Hitler announced that the SA would be sent on leave for the whole of July. Roehm replied with, 'The SA is and remains the destiny of Germany.'

On June 17th, von Papen showed political courage for the first time by making a speech at the University of Marburg demanding the end of the Nazi Terror and the return of freedom for the press. Hitler poured scorn on the 'pygmy' and instructed Goebbels to suppress publication of von Papen's speech wherever possible. Von Papen retaliated with his final attempt to exploit Hindenburg's confidence. When Hitler visited the President on June 21st, he found General von Blomberg there, who told him that Hindenburg threatened martial law if the state of tension was not eased. Action had become crucial. Himmler and Goering manufactured evidence of an imminent SA *putsch*. On June 28th, Roehm was expelled from the German Officers' League. On the 29th, Blomberg pledged Army support for Hitler in the *Völkischer Beobachter*. Goebbels threw in his influence against Roehm. Hitler, deceptively absent at a hotel on the Rhine at Godesberg, decided on action.

At 2 a.m. on the morning of June 30th, Hitler took off from an airfield near Bonn and flew to Munich. Shortly after dawn a long column of cars arrived at the hotel on the shores of the Tegernsee near Munich where Roehm and his friends were asleep. Hitler broke into Roehm's room and, in a state of frenzy, accused him of treachery. When Roehm refused the opportunity to shoot himself, he was shot while he stood at attention, stripped to the waist. Meanwhile SA leaders all over Germany were rounded up and shot by Himmler's SS. Many old scores were added to the death roll. Schleicher was shot as he answered the door. Gregor Strasser was taken to a Berlin gaol to die. Von Kahr, suppressor of the Munich *Putsch*, was found hacked to death by pickaxes in a swamp. Von Papen escaped but had to face the slaughter of his staff. Perhaps a thousand or more were killed by the afternoon of Sunday July 1st. By this time Hitler was acting as host in the Chancellery gardens at a tea party.

On the day after the slaughter had stopped, Hindenburg thanked Hitler and Goering for 'energetic action in suppressing high treason'. This was followed by General Blomberg's expression of the Cabinet's congratulations. The Army, pleased with how they had used Hitler, failed to notice that on July 26th Himmler was made *Reichsfuehrer* of an independent SS.

On August 2nd, Hindenburg died at the age of eighty-seven. At midday it was announced that the offices of Chancellor and President had been united in the person of Adolf Hitler, who also became Commander-in-Chief of the armed forces. A personal oath of allegiance to Hitler was extracted from all the armed forces. Hitler demanded a plebiscite to confirm his position. Oskar von Hindenburg broadcast a statement saying that his father had wished Hitler to succeed him. Von Papen kept silent about the edited Nazi version of Hindenburg's will that supported this.

On August 19th, 38,000,000 Germans, ninety per cent of the electorate, approved Hitler's seizure of power. Murderous tyranny was given the support of all but the 4,250,000 Germans who dared to vote 'No'.

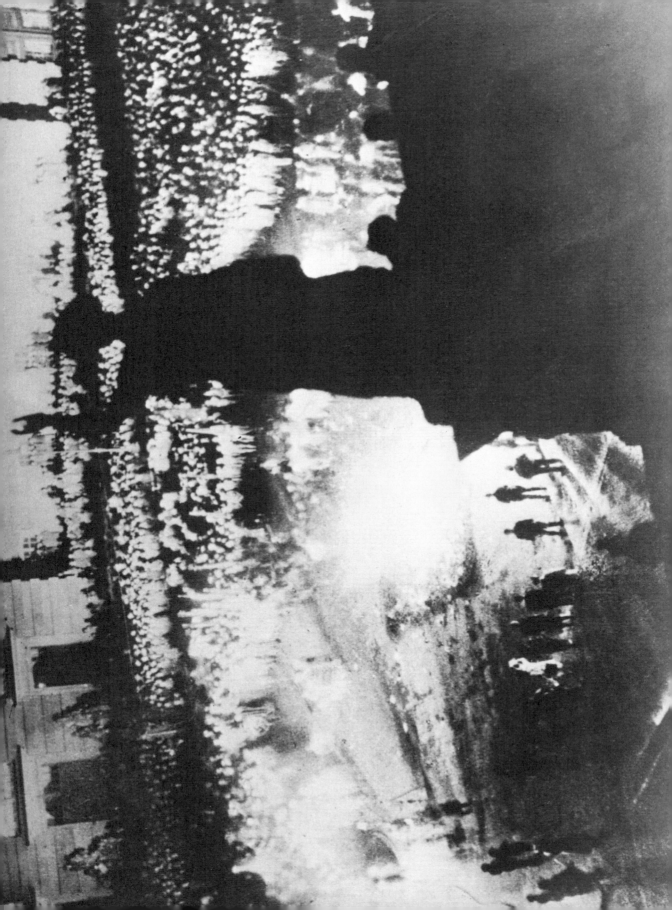

7

Life in
the Nazi State

The purge of the SA and the popular acceptance of Hitler's position as head of state completed his seizure of power over the political machinery of Germany. He was now faced with the challenge of the economic crisis and his desire to apply the Nazi revolution to German society as a whole. For both purposes Hitler introduced the term *Gleichschaltung* or 'Co-ordination'.

Hitler appreciated above all the need to restore confidence and a sense of energetic action to a people demoralised by unemployment and the collapse of security. He chose as his instrument Dr Schacht, President of the Reichsbank, who from the summer of 1934 became Minister of Economics. Schacht, although not a skilled politician, proved to be efficient in his handling of economics. The first target was unemployment. Nearly one million men were found at least temporary work in emergency building programmes, voluntary agricultural service and many semi-military enterprises. The armaments industry was encouraged to begin slow expansion.

The very gradual improvement in the world economy also had its effect. Unemployment fell from a peak of over six million to four million in December 1933, two and a quarter million in October 1934 and one million seven hundred thousand in August 1935. The return of confidence to the business world was achieved. Firms were given large incentives to invest

57

◄ The burning of 'degenerate' books, a frequent feature of the Nazi state capital. Employers were impressed by the state control of labour and the absence of strikes.

Schacht used his authority very skilfully. All economic decisions involving foreign currency were directed by him. Preference was given to the heavy industrial sector. Export subsidies made German prices artificially attractive overseas. Barter arrangements were introduced with economically weak countries in South America, Eastern Europe and the Balkans to avoid the loss of hard currency. Schacht was also helped by the generous settlement of international debts, particularly by Great Britain. The policies were a success. Between 1932 and 1937 both German national production and income rose by more than one hundred per cent. The Nazi slogan of 'Common Interest before Self Interest' appeared to have a strong foundation in fact. German workers joked about their lack of regret for the loss of the 'freedom to starve'.

Schacht's policies were not particularly Nazi, but as the government prospered so the nature of its programme became more obvious. As early as 1935, Schacht was directed to organise 'the economic preparations for war'. He himself wrote to Hitler, 'The accomplishment of the armaments programme with speed and in quantity is THE problem of German politics.' By 1937, Schacht became alarmed by the dimensions of the armaments programme required by Hitler and he resigned, handing over power to Hermann Goering as organiser of the Four Year Plan. Goering proved more suitable for Hitler's intentions, combining greater subservience with almost total ignorance of economic affairs. However, profits continued to expand for the larger businessmen. Between 1932 and 1938 undistributed profits rose from 175 million marks to 5,000 million marks. The price for this was greater and greater state control. Government regulations multiplied rapidly. Often only bribery could unlock the appropriate door to obtain official licences. As Dr Funk, Schacht's successor as Minister of Economics, admitted, 'For a single transaction as many as forty different forms must be filled out.' The disillusionment of German financiers is well illustrated by the flight of one of Hitler's early backers, Fritz Thyssen, in 1939. He later wrote, 'The Nazi regime has ruined German industry. What a *Dummkopf* (numbskull) I was!'

Thyssen was rich and clever enough to escape. Smaller figures fared much worse. A law of October 1937 dissolved all business corporations with a capital under £10,000. This effectively dissolved twenty per cent of small business firms. All employees were placed under the Labour Front, a Nazi organisation run by SA and SS members. In February 1935 a system of 'workbooks' was introduced which listed a worker's skills and determined how he could be employed and where. Workers were not consulted in wage disputes. The share of the working population in the national income between 1932 and 1938 fell by three per cent. In June 1936 the average working wage was estimated as around £2 per week and part of this was required for taxes and contributions to Nazi charities. Ironically, although heavy industry was the special interest of Nazi economic strategy, agriculture was perhaps the best organised ministry. Walther Darré, who became Minister of Food and Agriculture, knew his field well. He set out to maintain steady and profitable prices for the farmers and make Germany self-sufficient in food. His methods were characteristically Nazi. The farmer was given the honoured title of '*Bauer*' (peasant) provided he could prove his Aryan ancestry back to 1800. Agricultural prices were arbitrarily raised by twenty per cent. However, the immense feudal estates of the *Junkers* east of the Elbe remained in being. The *Bauer* was bound to the soil as firmly as a medieval peasant, although under the pressure of war production many successfully emigrated to the towns. In the long run Reich food production never exceeded eighty-three per cent of self-sufficiency. However, the State did provide heavily-subsidised cheap holidays, concerts and adult education courses. A week in the Bavarian Alps could cost as little as £3. Perhaps the greatest consideration that influenced the German worker was the sense that he had a secure job in a prospering state. As for most other Germans, economic security seemed to matter more than personal freedom.

The revival of economic confidence was the first essential Nazi achievement. The price included the control of all official organs of opinion. On May 10th 1933 a pile of 'degenerate' books was burnt in Berlin by cheering Nazi students opposite the University. The scene was repeated in several other cities. Henceforth all libraries were to be censored. The University of Berlin itself was put under the control of a new Rector, who was a member of the SA and a vet. He proceeded to introduce twenty-five new courses in racial science and, perhaps even more surprising, eighty-six in veterinology. All learning was given its Nazi approach. Professor Tomaschek, Director of the Institute of Physics at Dresden, was able to write, 'Modern Physics is an instrument of world Jewry for the destruction of Nordic Science.' Every person in the teaching profession was forced to join the National Socialists' Teachers League and swear an oath to be loyal and obedient to Adolf Hitler. University teachers had to spend six weeks in an observation camp to test their political reliability. By 1939 the number of university students was roughly forty per cent of those in 1933, and the chemical industry was complaining of the lack of qualified scientists. Most significant of all, Einstein, like his Italian counterpart Fermi, took his world-wide reputation to America. This probably did not trouble Hitler unduly for he was contemptuous of intellectuals and their failure to appreciate that, 'It was the Aryan who laid the groundwork and erected the walls of every great structure in human culture.'

For Hitler in fact education was something quite other than the development of the mind for independent enquiry. He attached the greatest importance to the control of the youth organisations which were such a feature of German life. In 1932 some ten million youths belonged to the Reich Committee of German Youth Associations, of which 107,956 were in the Hitler Youth. In June 1933 Baldur von Schirach was named Youth Leader of the German Reich. He began by sending SA thugs to take over the offices of the German Youth Organisation. They then went on to offer violence to its President, Admiral von Trotha, a famous naval hero. By December 1st 1936, Hitler had outlawed the Catholic Youth Association, despite a specific promise to the Papacy not to do so. Henceforth, 'All German youth is organised within the Hitler Youth.'

Schirach within his limits did an efficient job. Children went through various stages of training from the age of six to eighteen years. Great emphasis was placed on the boyish enthusiasm for camping, sport and games of a military nature. These did not stop short of the real thing. The use of rifles and races carrying packs were commonplace. Even girls were enrolled in the Youth Maidens organisation and had some taste of military exercises. However, from the age of ten to eighteen girls were impressed with the duty of becoming healthy mothers of vigorous Nazi children. For both boys and girls progress in Nazi ideology was a required activity. At eighteen boys and girls did Labour Service, often on the land. A select few might qualify for special schools, run by the SS, or the Order Castles at the very top of Nazi training. These involved nostalgic recall of the medieval Order of Teutonic Knights. After six years combining indoctrination in fanaticism with extremely rigorous physical training, a youth might reach the Order Castle in East Prussia near the Polish border, where particular emphasis was placed on the German need to expand into the land of the Slavs.

Undoubtedly Schirach did provide the Nazis with an unusually fit and enthusiastic core to their later armies. Particularly fine specimens were

Members of the Hitler Youth were encouraged to ▶
see themselves as the warriors of tomorrow

often sent as an advance guard into newly-acquired territories for propaganda purposes. Not without some justification could Hitler boast in November 1933, 'When an opponent declares "I will not come over to your side," I calmly say, "Your child belongs to us already."'

No precautions were spared to make sure that adults without the advantage of training in the Hitler Youth should receive healthy opinions and tastes. All Berlin newspaper editors and correspondents had daily meetings with Dr Goebbels or one of his assistants. Telegrams were dispatched to provincial papers and magazines. The radio was also strictly supervised. Films and theatres became particularly depressing organs of propaganda. The President of the Reich Theatre Chamber was one Hans Johst, famous for the remark 'When I hear the word culture, I reach for my revolver.' The hissing of films by German audiences became a commonplace. Goebbels was, however, a propagandist of subtlety. Some newspapers like the *Frankfurter Zeitung* and his own *Das Reich* were allowed a more liberal slant, and this no doubt increased their propaganda value with foreign readers.

Some of Goebbels' and Hitler's views on artistic matters were based on genuine conviction. Hitler regarded himself as an authority on architecture and delighted in massive pseudo-classical buildings. Both Hitler and Goebbels deplored art more modern than the Impressionists. Hitler personally supervised the works prepared for the Reich Chamber of Art, some of which aroused such fury in him that he kicked holes in them with his jackboot. Goebbels seems to have been genuinely surprised when his deliberately ill-sited exhibition of decadent painters like Kokoschka, Van Gogh, Matisse and Picasso proved so successful that it had to be hurriedly closed. Music remained the Nazi showcase. Although the works of such Jewish composers as Mendelssohn and Hindemith were barred, great figures like the conductor Furtwängler, composer Richard Strauss and the pianist Gieseking remained as champions of German culture. The Berlin Philharmonic Orchestra and State Opera were of the highest standard. Hitler professed enormous enthusiasm for the works of Wagner. He never missed a Wagner festival at Bayreuth and claimed to have heard *Götterdammerung* more than a hundred times.

Hitler and Goebbels were sufficiently confident of the success of the Nazi state to allow a surprising degree of freedom to travel. Only a few thousand were prohibited from travelling abroad. Tourists were encouraged and brought in valuable currency. The 1936 Olympic Games was a masterpiece of propaganda. The facilities were lavish and well-organised. Foreign visitors were offered spectacular entertainment. The only serious blemish to Nazi plans was the remarkable success of the American Negro athlete, Jesse Owens, whose four wins caused Hitler to leave the stadium in a temper.

Great outdoor displays were a Nazi speciality. The year was frequently punctuated with festivals, from the commemoration of the seizure of power on January 30th to that of those who fell in the Munich *Putsch* on November 9th. Perhaps the most spectacular of all were the Nuremberg rallies in September. Thousands were subjected to the minutely planned excitement of mass emotion. Superbly disciplined marching was accompanied by crescendoes of stirring music. Burning torches and hundreds of flags created the impression of a host united in a sacred cause. Searchlights carved splendid patterns from the night sky. Everything led up to the dramatic pause before the arrival of the *Fuehrer* (Leader) which was the signal for frenzied applause. Hitler's genius for the intoxication of a vast audience was given an unrivalled setting.

The ever-increasing power of the state was however also employed for much darker aims than obedience to the *Fuehrer* and the purification of culture. This last phrase came to mean steadily worsening treatment of the Jews. As early as 1933 they had been excluded from public office, the civil service, journalism, radio, farming, teaching, theatre and films. By 1938 a steady stream of laws had made their exclusion from society complete. Perhaps the most pernicious laws were those of Nuremberg in 1935. Jews were excluded from full citizenship. The marriage of Jews and Gentiles was banned. The employment of Aryan girls under thirty-five years of age was forbidden to Jews. However, the strictures of the law were not the worst experiences the Jews had to endure. They were entirely deprived of the protection of the law. Harassment supported by Nazi thugs was encouraged. Shops were stoned and offices wrecked. It was often difficult for Jews to get supplies of food. All over Germany notices appeared declaring, 'Jews not welcome here.' Perhaps the most perverse of many slogans was a sign at a sharp bend in the road near Ludwigshafen which read, 'Drive Carefully! Sharp Curve! Jews 75 m.p.h!'

Individual acts of brutality were given the final sanction of government support in the terrible week beginning after the Party Rally of November 9th 1938. On November 7th a seventeen-year-old German Jewish refugee, crazed by the deportation of his father to Poland, shot the third secretary of the German Embassy in Paris. As a reprisal Dr Goebbels ordered that

'spontaneous demonstrations' were to occur. The SS organised an orgy of violence and destruction. Nearly two hundred synagogues were subject to arson. At least 7,500 shops were wrecked and looted. Several Jews were shot while trying to escape death from burning. Many others were arrested and directed to concentration camps. In all the damage was estimated at some 25,000,000 marks. Insurance due to the Jews was confiscated by the State, and they were then subjected to a fine of one billion marks for their 'abominable crimes'. The true face of Nazi ideology was revealed to the world.

The Jewish faith was not the only one to incur Hitler's displeasure. He was also aware of the considerable prestige enjoyed by the Christian Church. In July 1933 Hitler had signed a *Concordat* with the Pope guaranteeing the Catholic Church freedom and the right to run its own affairs. This apparent Papal sanction of Hitler's regime provided a useful propaganda effect. In practice Hitler detested the existence of rival creeds and pursued a policy of persistent intimidation combined with protestations of respect. By March 1937 the Pope was sufficiently disillusioned to issue the encyclical 'With Burning Sorrow'.

The forty-five million Protestants suffered from the fact that they were split up into some thirty different sects. Also some of their leaders, even Pastor Niemoeller, who was later to be one of Hitler's most outspoken critics, began by welcoming the Nazis as an alternative to Weimar backed by Catholics and Socialists. They soon learnt the mistake they had made. The Nazi element among them became organised as the 'German Christians' led by Ludwig Mueller. The Nazis let loose a characteristic wave of intimidation to ensure Mueller's election as Reich Bishop. The contradictions involved in combining Christ's teaching with Nazi ideology soon became all too obvious. Niemoeller challenged Mueller by setting up an alternative Confessional Church with its own organisation. The Secret Police arrested several hundred Confessional Church pastors, confiscated their funds and murdered one of their leaders in Sachsenhausen concentration camp. Niemoeller was arrested after an outspoken sermon. After eight months he was fined two thousand marks and sentenced to seven months imprisonment for abuse of the pulpit. As he left the court, he was taken into 'protective custody' by the Secret Police and spent the next seven years in a concentration camp.

Some true indication of Nazi intentions was revealed in the wartime programme for the 'National Reich Church'. Its articles included instructions that, 'The National Church will clear away from its altars all cruci-

65

Himmler takes a salute as leader of the SS

fixes, Bibles and pictures of saints. On the altars there must be nothing but *Mein Kampf* (to the German nation and therefore to God the most sacred book) and to the left of the altar a sword. The National Church demands immediate cessation of the publishing and distribution of the Bible.'

The plain fact was that after the purge of the SA in June 1934 considerations of law and freedom were valueless. As early as March 1933 political crimes had been allocated to special courts. However, the main instrument of terror was the Gestapo or Secret State Police. Goering originally created this force in April 1933 for special acts of intimidation in Prussia. Its expansion began a year later when it came under the control of Himmler. Assisted by Heydrich, who organised the Intelligence Branch, the Gestapo became the most feared force ever known. Rash words or actions could lead to the dreaded knock on the door, often in the middle of the night, which entailed arrest for 'protective custody'. This was a typical Nazi phrase, combining apparent legality with the practice of barbarism. The concentration camps became centres of murder and callous degradation. By the end of 1933 there were already fifty of them. In the nineteen-thirties their total population never exceeded 30,000, but their crucial role, as Himmler saw, was the terror they inspired.

As in society as a whole so also in government, all authority stemmed from Hitler. The Law for the Protection of the People and the Enabling Act, both passed in 1933, gave him all the authority he needed. The Reichstag became a sounding board for Hitler's speeches. It met only twelve times and passed only four laws in the six years before 1939. The Cabinet met rarely and never after February 1938. Even the Reich Defence Council met only twice. Hitler's practice was to appoint special departments under picked leaders. There were eventually forty-two executive departments, often overlapping in their activities. Hitler delighted in the rivalry this caused and revelled in his role as supreme arbiter in disputes between figures as prominent as Schacht and Goering, or Neurath, his Foreign Minister, and Ribbentrop, who ran his own foreign affairs bureau. The vast complex of an ever-multiplying bureaucracy, living in fear of the Gestapo, was at the disposal of one man, the *Fuehrer*.

Despite the loss of personal freedom, most Germans seem at first to have been pleased with Nazi rule. The liberal historian Alan Bullock has written, 'No German Government since Bismarck's had enjoyed such popular support as Hitler's.' Millions of Germans were prepared to accept his claim to be the saviour of their country. Perhaps the secret lay in Hitler's appeal to what Friedrich Meinecke has called a sense of '*Volk*', a view of the German nation specially distinguished from other peoples. More practically, the return of economic prosperity closed many minds. Moreover, once Hitler had mastered Germany itself, he turned his attention to foreign policy. For five years the people applauded his triumphs in plebiscites, which usually registered over ninety-five per cent approval. This figure may have owed a little to the fact that the Gestapo had devised a way of detecting those who voted against Hitler, but undoubtedly it was based on real enthusiasm.

8

Peace and Triumph

After 1934, Hitler was content more and more to leave internal affairs in Germany to trusted colleagues such as Goering, Himmler and Goebbels. His energies were directed to the aim which he had described in *Mein Kampf* and repeated in almost every speech since, the destruction of the Treaty of Versailles. His methods in foreign policy were similar to those he had used so effectively against his opponents inside Germany. Acts of violence and threats of more were accompanied by protestations of good intention. Whereas at home on the way to power he had continually stressed his concern for democratic procedure, he now began to lecture the statesmen of Europe on the principles of Versailles, his interest in the rights of nations to self-determination and above all his longing for peace.

Hitler's first step in the programme outlined in *Mein Kampf* almost began with a false move. Since coming to power, Hitler had encouraged the development of an Austrian Nazi party with money for explosives and weapons and facilities inside Germany for exiled leaders. On July 25th 1934 these efforts appeared to be bringing results. A group of Nazis broke into the Austrian Chancellery and fatally wounded Chancellor Dolfuss. Vienna's radio station was seized and the resignation of Dolfuss announced. However, the Austrian Nazis were badly organised and the revolt was quickly put down by forces led by Dr Kurt von Schuschnigg.

Hitler was caught unawares. He had been at the opera at the Bayreuth festival when the news of Dolfuss' shooting began to come through. Later that night, Hitler realised that the *coup* was doomed to failure. The news that a 'Greater Germany' was about to be formed was suppressed. The murderers of Dolfuss were condemned. Hitler declared the matter purely an Austrian affair. A little later we find him in an interview to the *Daily Mail* emphasising that, 'Germany's problems cannot be settled by war,' and in one with a French veteran recalling the horrors they had both experienced in trench warfare.

How little these assurances were worth is shown by the fact that on October 1st 1934, Hitler gave his orders for the Army to treble its size, the Navy to start building submarines and larger battle cruisers and for an Air Force to be developed. The chemical combine I. G. Farben was instructed to push ahead plans for the development of synthetic oil and rubber. All these preparations were to be veiled with secrecy. The German army rank lists were no longer published. Pilots were to be trained under cover of the League of Air Sports. The machinery of war was put into motion. Hitler waited until an opportunity occurred to exploit his new strength in the world of diplomacy.

In January 1935 the Saar voted overwhelmingly for a return to the Reich by 477,000 votes to 48,000. The British and French, who were more aware of the extent of German rearmament than Hitler realised, instead of threatening to halt it began to throw out feelers for a general settlement of European problems, especially those in Eastern Europe. The proposals went so far as to offer arms equality for Germany. On March 10th Goering admitted in an interview the existence of the Air Force. Hitler waited, but no significant reaction occurred. Encouraged by this, on March 16th Hitler announced the trebling of the armed forces and the return of military service. The following day, Heroes' Memorial Day, developed into a celebration of the successful defiance of Versailles. At the State Opera House a throng of uniforms flaunted the return of military confidence. They ranged from the faded splendour of the Death's Head Hussars on the Kaiser's last surviving Field Marshal, von Mackensen, to the new sky-blue of Goering's Air Force, the *Luftwaffe*.

Considering his lack of political and diplomatic experience—all Hitler's knowledge of England and France was second-hand—he showed a masterly insight into the attitude of the English and French governments. At Stresa they met with Italian diplomats to condemn Hitler. France, Russia and

Czechoslovakia signed treaties of mutual aid. The League of Nations set up a committee. All this led to no effective action. Hitler sensed straight away that the Western democracies, slowly recovering from the wounds inflicted by the depression and vividly aware of the horrors that war had already involved from 1914 to 1918, were in no mood for maintaining law by force. Furthermore, rather to his surprise, they seemed recklessly anxious to believe his claims of good intentions. On May 21st, Hitler made a long speech to the Reichstag decrying war and ending with, 'Germany needs and desires peace.' He announced solemnly lack of interest in Alsace–Lorraine or in union with Austria. He suggested plans for disarmament and that the German Navy should be limited to thirty-five per cent of the size of the British. The offer was rapidly seized upon. *The Times* declared approval. The British Government entered abruptly into a naval agreement with Germany, without informing either the League or her Stresa allies. The flimsy basis of international agreements was revealed for all to see. Furthermore the point was missed that thirty-five per cent of the British level meant full production for the German shipyards.

In October 1935 another event occurred which pleased Hitler. In a belated search for Empire, Italy attacked Abyssinia. The League voted economic sanctions, which proved ineffective. Hitler realised that whatever the result the Italians were bound to damage their relations with England and France. What could be more natural than that they should look towards Germany as an ally? Mindful that the presence of four Italian divisions at the Brenner Pass in 1934 had been among the reasons for disowning the Austrian Nazis, Hitler began assiduously to cultivate Italy as an ally.

Nineteen days before Hitler's speech protesting peaceful intentions, he had ordered General Blomberg to distribute plans among a few topmost officers for the reoccupation of the demilitarised Rhineland. The unusually well-informed French Ambassador in Berlin, François-Poncet, in November warned his government that Hitler intended to achieve this. The pretext for action was included in the 'Peace Speech'. Hitler had referred to the treaty between France and Russia as introducing an element of legal insecurity into international affairs.

On February 27th 1936 the French Chamber of Deputies confirmed the treaty. At dawn on March 7th a token force of roughly three German battalions crossed the bridges of the Rhine. At midday Hitler addressed the Reichstag. His announcement of the movement of troops was greeted with a

Preparations for war. Hitler and General Blomberg attend Army manoeuvres in 1937

roar of hysterical applause. Only the generals looked worried. They knew that the French were capable of mobilising up to one hundred divisions. As Hitler later admitted, 'If the French had then marched into the Rhineland, we would have had to withdraw with our tails between our legs.' Blomberg had in fact made arrangements for just such a withdrawal. The military action was however combined with an astute political move. On the same day that the troops moved in, the German Foreign Minister, Neurath, handed the British, French and Italian ambassadors Hitler's latest peace proposals. The plausible myth was established that Germany was 're-occupying her back garden'.

The bait worked. Britain's Foreign Secretary, Anthony Eden, told the House of Commons, 'We have no reason to suppose that Germany's present action threatens hostilities.' The French would not move without British backing. Against the advice of all his experts, Hitler had decisively altered the balance of power in Europe. When he dissolved the Reichstag and asked

71

NORWAY
OSLO
SWEDEN
STOCKHOLM
DENMARK
COPENHAGEN
BALTIC SEA
MEMELLAND
LITHUANIA
GREAT BRITAIN
Danzig
EAST PRUSSIA
LONDON
HOLLAND
BERLIN
WARSAW
BRUSSELS
BELGIUM
POLAND
RHINELAND
G E R M A N Y
PARIS
SAAR
SUDETENLAND
PRAGUE
TESCHEN
F R A N C E
CZECHOSLOVAKIA
SWITZ.
A U S T R I A
VIENNA
HUNGARY
BUDAPEST
VICHY FRANCE
RUM
MADRID
Danube
BELGRADE
S P A I N
YUGOSLAVIA
BU
I T A L Y
ROME
Monte Cassino
Anzio
ALBANIA
Naples
GREECE
M E D I T E R Salerno
GIBRALTAR
ATHEN
ALGIERS
R A N E A N
MOROCCO
SICILY
ALGERIA
TUNIS
MALTA
TUNISIA
Tripoli
TRIPOLI
Tobru
LIBYA
CYRENAIC

0   500 MILES
0   800 KM

HITLER'S GAINS BEFORE OCTOBE

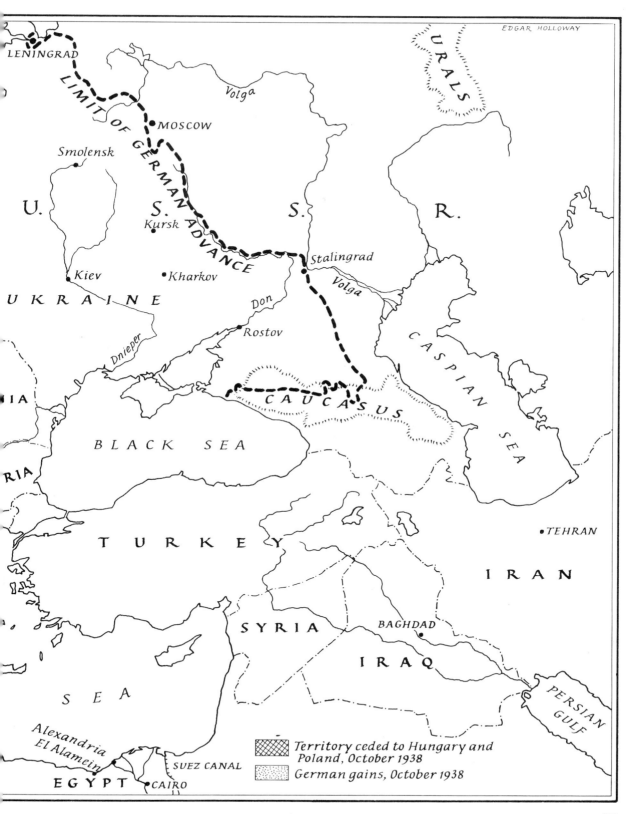

EDGAR HOLLOWAY

LENINGRAD

URALS

Volga

LIMIT OF GERMAN ADVANCE

MOSCOW

Smolensk

U.   S.   S.   R.

Kursk

Kiev   •Kharkov   Stalingrad

U K R A I N E   *Volga*

Don   CASPIAN

Dnieper   Rostov   SEA

C A U C A S U S

BLACK   SEA

•TEHRAN

T U R K E Y   I R A N

SYRIA   BAGHDAD

IRAQ

SEA   PERSIAN

Alexandria   GULF
El Alamein

SUEZ CANAL

E G Y P T   •CAIRO

▨ Territory ceded to Hungary and
      Poland, October 1938
░ German gains, October 1938

for a referendum to approve his action, 98·8 per cent of Germans gave him their support.

Hitler concentrated his energies for the next year on improving his diplomatic position. Events outside Germany helped him considerably. On July 4th 1936, the League admitted the failure of its sanctions against Italy and withdrew them. The possibility arose of better relations between Italy and France and Britain. Barely a fortnight later civil war broke out in Spain and the Italian dictator, Mussolini, at once committed large-scale support to the Fascist commander, Franco. The French were seriously alarmed by the prospect of another Fascist neighbour. In the same month Hitler negotiated an agreement with Austria which promised no intervention in each other's internal affairs. The main cause of possible friction with Italy seemed to have been removed. Hitler sent a small force to Spain as a useful training ground, but deliberately refrained from intervention decisive enough to bring a quick end to the war. However, the terror bombing by his Condor Legion of the undefended Spanish town of Guernica created a wave of apprehensive horror in the peace-loving democracies.

Meanwhile German rearmament was accelerated and diplomatic siege was laid to Italy. In October 1936, the Italian Foreign Minister, Ciano, was invited to Munich. In January, May and June 1937 German ambassadors visited Italy. Finally on September 23rd, Mussolini set out for Munich in a specially designed new uniform. He was treated to a magnificently organised display of German might: Army manoeuvres at Mecklenberg, the massive production of the Krupp factories, and eight hundred thousand Party members roaring their applause at a mass meeting in Berlin. Hitler even went so far as to describe Mussolini as 'one of those lonely men who are the makers of history'. Three weeks later Mussolini added his signature to the Anti-Comintern pact Germany had made with Japan. Hitler made much of Germany's role as a bulwark against Bolshevik Russia. Repeated assurances were also given to Poland of Germany's peaceful intentions towards her. Goering pledged his word that Germany had no interest either in Danzig or the Polish Corridor. It remained to be seen to what aims this diplomacy was directed.

In July 1937 Blomberg had already circulated three copies of a 'Top Secret' document to the heads of the armed forces. It listed war possibilities and included attacks on both Austria and Czechoslovakia as well as preparations for a struggle in the West. On November 5th Hitler summoned to the Reich Chancellery his three Commanders-in-Chief, Blomberg the War

Minister and Neurath the Foreign Minister. Hitler's adjutant Colonel Hossbach took the minutes. Hitler talked for four hours and reviewed his ideas of Germany's position. He stressed the lack of self-sufficient food supply and basic raw materials. He gave as his solution the necessity of increased '*Lebensraum*' or 'Living Space'. The question was where could Germany make greatest gains at the lowest cost? He emphasised the necessity of the use of force. He pointed out that German strength would be at its peak in the years up to 1943, after which the Western powers might expect to catch up. He analysed possible weaknesses in France and England which would make war likely to succeed. In all events the occupation of Austria and Czechoslovakia was essential to protect Germany's southern and eastern flanks. Despite all the praise for peace, Hitler's essential aims outlined in *Mein Kampf* remained intact. The commanders were amazed. Blomberg, Fritsch the Army Commander and Neurath all expressed doubt of Germany's preparedness for a major war.

Hitler's self-confidence was now reaching new heights. Encouraged by his colleagues Goering and Himmler, Hitler became increasingly impatient of expert advice. In December 1937 Schacht had resigned as Minister of Economics in protest against Goering's reckless expenditure on armaments. Neurath had dared to question Hitler's strategy and was replaced by Ribbentrop, arrogant and tactless but a devoted disciple of the *Fuehrer*. The last remaining citadel of independence was the Army. Here chance provided Hitler with an opportunity which he exploited ruthlessly. Field Marshal Blomberg made the unfortunate mistake of marrying his secretary, who was later discovered to have a police record as a prostitute. When the Army Command demanded Blomberg's resignation, Hitler explained that he was obliged to dismiss the Field Marshal until the scandal died down. General Fritsch, Commander-in-Chief of the Army, was suddenly faced with an informer produced by Himmler, who claimed to have evidence of a homosexual offence committed by the General. Having previously given his word that the charge was untrue, Fritsch maintained outraged silence.

On February 4th Hitler addressed his Cabinet at what was to be its last meeting and announced that in future he would become Commander-in-Chief of the armed forces. The War Ministry was to be replaced by a separate High Command of the Armed Forces (OKW), which became Hitler's personal staff. Goering's ambitions were satisfied by promotion to Field Marshal and the highest rank in the Reich. Fritsch, whose retirement was attributed to ill-health, was later fully exonerated. By then, however, the

Fuehrer was in unassailable command. For good measure sixty senior officers were either retired or transferred. The ambassadors in Rome, Tokyo and Vienna were dismissed. The last of these was von Papen and his reaction was to have dramatic results.

Von Papen was informed of his dismissal on the telephone by a state secretary. He was greatly surprised, having seen Hitler only a week before and no doubt disclosed the Austrian Nazi plan for a *coup* in the spring of 1938. He hurried to the Berghof, Hitler's mountain retreat near Munich, to see Hitler, officially to make his farewell, in practice no doubt to assess his own future. In the course of an embarrassing interview, he mentioned that the Austrian Chancellor Schuschnigg would favour a personal conversation with Hitler. Hitler seized on this idea and ordered von Papen to resume his post and organise the visit.

Having been assured that the Austro–German agreement of 1936 would be the basis of discussion, on February 11th Schuschnigg set out to meet Hitler at the Berghof. He was surprised to be greeted by Hitler in uniform and flanked by generals. Once they were alone in Hitler's study, the *Fuehrer* began a violent harangue, beginning, 'The whole history of Austria is one uninterrupted act of high treason,' and ending with the offer of signing an ultimatum that afternoon of which no details were given.

The ultimatum proved to involve an amnesty for Austrian Nazis and the placing of the Ministries of the Interior and of War in Nazi hands. Proposals were also made for the interrelation of the Austrian and German armies and economies. Hitler bluntly told Schuschnigg, 'You will fulfil my demands in three days or I will order the march into Austria.' The most Schuschnigg could obtain was three days' grace to carry out the agreement. Faced by threats and very real German troop movements, Schuschnigg and the Austrian President, Miklas, agreed to implement the German terms. However, the Germans were not satisfied. The Austrian Nazis let loose a wave of terrorism which threatened Schuschnigg's control of his own country. He decided on a last act of defiance. He proposed a plebiscite on Austrian independence to take place on Sunday March 13th. Hitler was for once caught off his guard and reacted furiously. On Thursday March 10th he decided on action. Orders were given to mobilise the Army. Prince Philip of Hesse was sent to seek Mussolini's support. Instructions were sent to the Austrian Nazi, Seyss-Inquart, who had become Minister of the Interior.

On March 11th, Schuschnigg was wakened early with the news that the frontier had been closed. Soon after lunch that day he told Seyss-Inquart

◀ A Reichstag ovation triumphantly endorses
Hitler's occupation of Austria

Viennese Jews are made to scrub the street, 1938, surrounded by
jeering Nazis

that he agreed to postpone the plebiscite. Goering then telephoned to
demand Schuschnigg's resignation and replacement by Seyss-Inquart.
Nazi demonstrators began to fill the centre of Vienna. In the evening
Schuschnigg broadcast the news of the German ultimatum and denied the
danger of civil war. Goering demanded that Seyss-Inquart should ask for
German help 'to prevent bloodshed'. Just before midnight President
Miklas agreed to Seyss-Inquart's appointment as Chancellor. He rang up to
say that German aid was no longer needed, only to find that the troops were
already moving in. The order seems to have been given even before Hitler
learnt that Mussolini promised his support. Shortly after lunch Hitler
himself crossed the border into Austria. Much to his delight, as he travelled
towards his childhood home, Linz, Hitler was greeted with cheering crowds
and hastily collected flags. This seems to have decided him in favour of
taking over Austria completely. Seyss-Inquart was hurried off to Vienna

and after a cabinet meeting was able by Sunday night to present Hitler with a law which began 'Austria is a province of the Third Reich.' Hitler spent Monday in the Hofburg, palace of the Austrian emperors.

The next month was spent on making sure of the popular applause which was Hitler's trump card. He travelled all over Germany and for ten days in Austria. On the eve of the vote he broadcast a speech from Vienna which ended, 'Tomorrow may every German bow in humility before the Almighty who in a few weeks has wrought a miracle upon us.' Both the Germans and Austrians voted support of over ninety-nine per cent. Although many Austrians genuinely welcomed union with the Reich with its power and promise of work, the support for Hitler must have owed something to its lack of secrecy. Moreover, Himmler and the Gestapo were already at work. In Vienna alone some seventy thousand arrests occurred in the first month and Austria was given the benefit of its own concentration camp at Mauthausen.

After Austria, who would be next? This was the question that now occupied European governments. German armaments had more than doubled in three years. Throughout that period the Nazis had been subsidising the Nazi Sudeten Party in Czechoslovakia. Two weeks after entering Austria, Hitler instructed the leader of the Sudeten Nazis to start making unacceptable demands upon the Czech government.

Czechoslovakia had been the creation of Versailles. It was a mixture of Czechs, Slovaks, Germans, Ruthenians and Hungarians. Despite considerable progress towards democracy and the development of a fine army backed by the renowned Skoda arms works, the Czech government had faced continued difficulty with its three and a quarter million German minority. As recently as the end of 1937 the Czechs had tried to develop some new understanding with the Sudeten Germans. At the end of April 1938, the British and French urged the Czechs to make maximum concessions to them.

Hitler meanwhile enjoyed himself in Italy on a state visit where every effort was made to display the splendour and strength of the two countries. Rumours continued of German troop movements and intentions. On May 20th Benes, the Czech leader, surprised the Germans by ordering partial mobilisation of the army. To Hitler's amazement, the British and French followed this up with severe warnings of the possible results of aggression against the Czechs. Hitler was furious, but for the time being he was obliged to assure the Czech ambassador that Germany had no aggressive intentions.

On May 30th Hitler signed a military directive 'to smash Czechoslovakia' in the near future. When the generals led by General Beck met and tried to persuade Hitler of the dangers of war, he raved at them, 'It is my un-shakeable will that Czechoslovakia shall be wiped off the map.' September 27th at noon was fixed as the deadline for the attack.

Hitler's plans were now influenced by the actions of Neville Chamberlain, the British Prime Minister, who was firmly convinced that he could per-suade Hitler to be reasonable. On September 7th *The Times* published a leading article suggesting the cession of the Sudetenland to Germany. On September 12th Hitler made a violent attack on President Benes in his speech at the Nuremberg Rally. Chamberlain was not dismayed and the next day suggested a personal visit to Hitler. On the 15th Chamberlain flew to the Berghof and after undergoing a full review of Hitler's justification for his policies succeeded in getting his assurance that he would wait to see if Chamberlain could get agreement to the peaceful cession of the Sudeten-land.

A week later, Chamberlain was again flying to Hitler at Godesberg with just such an agreement from the British, French and Czech governments. Hitler then demanded occupation by the German army before a plebiscite could be held. The Czechs mobilised. On Chamberlain's return, the British cabinet rejected Hitler's terms. On September 26th Hitler lost control of himself at a speech in the Sports Palace and heaped abuse on Benes. War seemed certain.

Hitler, however, was momentarily checked by several disappointments. The Berlin crowds showed no enthusiasm for war, and turned their backs on a mechanised division parading through the streets. Hitler received warning of near total French mobilisation and almost total Italian failure to react. The British fleet took up battle stations. The Czech army was almost equal in size to the German. Hitler wrote to Chamberlain, leaving the door just open for negotiations. Chamberlain announced this to a cheering Commons. Mussolini backed the idea of a conference, and on September 29th Hitler, Chamberlain, Mussolini and Daladier, the French Premier, met at Munich and agreed to dismember Czechoslovakia. Germany gained 11,000 square miles, the excellent Czech system of fortifications and well over half its industrial materials. Chamberlain flew back to London, brandishing a sheet of paper, an Anglo–German agreement never to go to war again, and promising, 'Peace in our time.' The Czech Foreign Minister declared, 'Today it is our turn, tomorrow it will be the turn of others.'

81

◄ Chamberlain, Daladier, Hitler, Mussolini and
Ciano achieve uneasy agreement at Munich

Undoubtedly throughout Europe there was a strong desire for peace. The crowds in Munich and London cheered Chamberlain. When Winston Churchill told the Commons, 'We have sustained a total, unmitigated defeat,' he was shouted down. After the excitement died, probably a majority of British people felt that Chamberlain was right to regard the union of the Sudeten Germans with Germany as a poor motive for war. Hitler, however, was not satisfied. He was appalled by the German enthusiasm for peace and on return from Munich told his SS bodyguard, 'That fellow Chamberlain has ruined my entry into Prague.' He waited for a further opportunity to exploit the weakness of those he called 'the little worms' of Munich.

The British were determined not to be found so weak again. The attacks on the Jews in the terrible pogrom of November 1938 horrified public opinion in Great Britain and America. Rearmament in Britain began to develop more rapidly than in Germany.

In March 1939 crisis again flared up in Czechoslovakia. The Slovaks rebelled against the Czechs, spurred on by Nazi incitement, and Hitler promised to guarantee Slovak independence. Chamberlain declared that Britain was no longer bound to guarantee the frontiers of Czechoslovakia. The German papers soon began to fill with stories of Czech atrocities against German minorities in Bohemia and Moravia. When the Czech President and Foreign Minister flew to Berlin to try to prevent German action, they were subjected to the same intimidation as the Austrian Chancellor. Goering threatened to destroy Prague from the air. The President was left with the choice of signing away his country or causing its destruction by force. He chose to sign. A *communiqué* announced that the President had invited the *Fuehrer* to take the Czech people under the protection of the German Reich to safeguard calm, order and peace.

At dawn on March 15th 1939 German troops marched into Bohemia and Moravia. That night Hitler slept in the palace of the Kings of Bohemia in Prague. He had the opportunity to gloat, 'I shall go down in history as the greatest German.'

9

War and Victory

The occupation of Prague, despite Hitler's statement after Munich that he had no more territorial claims to make, had a decisive effect on public opinion in England. Hitler was now widely regarded as a man whose word could never be trusted. Feelings were particularly strong in the Conservative Party, the party led by Neville Chamberlain. It was known that the Germans had already begun to make demands on Poland. Barely a fortnight after Hitler occupied Czechoslovakia, Chamberlain told the Commons that the British Government was determined to guarantee Polish independence. A week later, on April 6th, this guarantee was endorsed in a pact in which the English and French promised assistance to Poland in case of attack. The very next day Italy attacked Albania and appeared to confirm the view of the Fascist powers as hungry for plunder. On April 26th, Great Britain introduced limited conscription, the first time this had ever happened in peacetime.

In fact Hitler's policy had not suddenly changed. As early as November 1937 he had explained to his generals his plans for extending German living space and the necessity for the occupation of Austria and Czechoslovakia. However, as his policy of combining threats of force with the building up of tension and the profession of lawful aims brought results, so Hitler's confidence steadily increased. It is not possible to be certain what his exact intentions were towards Poland. The separation of East Prussia from Germany and the insistence that the German city of Danzig was a free port contributing profit to the Poles was a long-standing grievance among German nationalists. Hitler was not personally so angry as many of his people. He had signed an alliance with the Poles, and when he had dismembered Czechoslovakia, Poland had joined in and seized the Teschen district.

Hitler began by trying diplomacy. In October 1938, Ribbentrop told the Polish Ambassador over lunch at Berchtesgaden that the Germans were interested in a settlement of mutual differences, and that this would involve the return of Danzig to the Reich and the establishment of a German road and rail link with East Prussia across the Polish Corridor. The Polish Foreign Minister, Colonel Beck, was determined that Poland would not be another Czechoslovakia. He thought that the only way to prevent further diplomatic demands was to make a determined stand and say, 'No!' By November 24th, Hitler had issued an order to his generals to be ready for the sudden occupation of Danzig. The early months of 1939 were taken up with the Czech crisis, but this was immediately followed by an event with sinister overtones for the Poles. Hitler compelled Lithuania to return Memelland to East Prussia to redress its wrongful loss under the Treaty of Versailles.

Hitler certainly does not seem to have been unduly perturbed by English and French diplomacy. On April 3rd he issued his commanders with orders that included the invasion of Poland beginning on September 1st. On April 28th in a major speech to the Reichstag, Hitler poured scorn on the American President's demand for a guarantee of peaceful intentions. He also renounced the German–Polish Agreement of 1934 and the Anglo–German Naval Agreement of 1935. In May Germany and Italy signed the Pact of Steel, proclaiming mutual assistance in the securing of living space or in case of war. The Italians tried to slow Hitler down by extracting a promise of no war before 1942. On the day after signing this pact, Hitler explained to his fourteen main military leaders that Danzig was only one objective in the search for living space. 'We are left with the decision to attack Poland at the first suitable opportunity.'

The focus of attention on Poland left England and France with the uncomfortable realisation of their difficulty in giving any assistance to distant Poland. They began to seek some understanding with Soviet Russia. Unfortunately many English and French politicians regarded Russia as

Heinkel He 111s, the bombers that brought terror ▶
to the skies of Europe in 1939 and 1940

almost as great a menace as Germany. The years 1935–8 had witnessed terrible purges inside Russia. The countries lying between Germany and Russia were extremely reluctant to allow the movement of Russian troops across their soil. The Russians at first seemed anxious for an alliance but became increasingly suspicious of Anglo–French caution. By August the negotiations were deadlocked. The Germans seized their chance. They offered the Russians not only a non-aggression pact but secret terms for the partition of Poland. The Russians seem to have decided in favour of achieving their own immediate profit and perhaps a better position to resist later German attacks. On August 24th, Ribbentrop and Molotov produced their bombshell, a German–Russian agreement neither to attack nor assist in attack on one another during the next ten years.

While Ribbentrop was in Moscow, Hitler once more addressed his generals. He told them to be ready for war on August 26th. He stressed that it was now the Army's turn to provide a military triumph to equal his political one, and that in making war it was victory not right that mattered. He also promised a good propaganda reason for starting the war. A lukewarm effort was made to achieve British neutrality. Hitler also offered Poland terms which could only mean its destruction without fighting. The British were now determined to stand by Poland. The one piece of news that caused Hitler to hesitate was Mussolini's warning that Italy was quite unprepared for war and needed massive supplies of raw materials. Hitler postponed the date of the attack until September 1st. He spent the week preparing the German people, who remained remarkably unenthusiastic for war, for the need to resist Polish provocation. Meanwhile drugged criminals were dressed in Polish uniforms and on the evening of August 31st shot and photographed near Polish frontier posts to provide the evidence to justify retaliation. At dawn on September 1st air attacks began.

Even when the shooting had started, the French and British governments still tried to persuade Mussolini to arrange a conference. English public opinion was furious. Chamberlain was obliged to issue an ultimatum. At 11 a.m. on September 3rd, Great Britain was at war with Germany and by the afternoon France had followed suit.

The invasion of Poland developed into a classic demonstration of the German technique of *Blitzkrieg* or lightning war. Massed forces of armour and mechanised infantry made rapid advances to encircle slow-moving troops. Aerial bombardment wrecked Polish supply routes. Faked broadcasts undermined morale and increased confusion. The Poles, despite brave and determined fighting, were overwhelmed. They were reduced to confronting tanks with cavalry. By September 19th, Hitler had driven across Poland to the Baltic and made a triumphant entry into Danzig. To his annoyance Warsaw stubbornly held out for another ten days. Even the German allies, the Russians, were surprised by the speed of victory. On September 17th, they began hurriedly to occupy their share of Eastern Poland. By October 5th, the remains of the Polish army had surrendered.

Five days after the Polish surrender, Hitler startled his generals by urging a late autumn or winter attack in the West. He emphasised the need for swift action in order to eliminate French resistance before Russia could possibly cause trouble in the East. The generals protested that they were not confident of smashing the French, particularly in view of the speed required in transferring forces from Poland. Some of them even got as far as detailed plans to remove Hitler. They came to nothing. Hitler established personal ascendancy over General Brauchitsch, the Commander-in-Chief of the Army, and the generals were reduced to producing technical reasons for postponing the attack. On January 20th 1940, which had been one of Hitler's proposed dates for attack, the arrest in Belgium of an officer carrying the full operational plans caused further delays.

The postponement of the attack in the West provided time for two additional schemes to attract Hitler's attention. First Admiral Raeder, Commander-in-Chief of the Navy, pointed out the desirability of securing iron supplies from Sweden. He suggested a surprise naval attack on Norway and Denmark to prevent any British intervention in that area. It was the kind of dramatic scheme that appealed to Hitler. On April 9th the invasion began. The Danes surrendered within twenty-four hours. The Norwegians were caught unawares by a series of naval landings at their ports. Despite brave resistance and some rather badly organised British help, central Norway was obliged to surrender by May 3rd. Resistance lasted a little longer in the north and Narvik was even temporarily recaptured by a British, Norwegian and French force, but by June 8th, German victory was complete.

The second scheme to interest Hitler was proposed by the Commander of German Army Group A, General von Rundstedt. He put forward the idea of combining the proposed attack through Holland and Belgium, which he judged correctly the English and French were expecting, with an even larger thrust through the Ardennes, on the weak hinge of the border between France and Belgium. If this was successful the bulk of the enemy could then be surrounded in Belgium. Hitler was delighted with the idea and added his own plans for parachute commandos to seize crucial strategic positions, bridges and forts. On Friday May 10th the attack began.

The winter had been well spent by the German commanders. Gliders and paratroops swept down on Holland and Belgium. Some landed right on top of the Belgian fortress of Eben-Emael. The Dutch forces were overrun. Undefended Rotterdam was pounded from the air. By the evening of May 14th, the Dutch had surrendered. The small British force of nine divisions and the pick of the French army moved into Belgium to meet what they took to be the main German thrust. When he heard the news, Hitler 'could have wept for joy'.

On 13th and 14th of May, a massive concentration of German armour began to advance through the wooded hills of the Ardennes protected by fighter planes. They were opposed by scattered Belgian units and an unimpressive French conscript army, which totally failed to exploit the extended nature of the German line of advance. Stuka dive bombers and Junker 88s brought terror to bear at crucial moments. By the end of May 14th, the Germans had crossed the Meuse near Sedan. Tanks and mechanised infantry began the dash for the sea. On May 20th they reached the Channel coast near Abbeville. The French forces had been cut in two. On May 27th the Belgians surrendered. The British, having attempted a tank attack on the exposed German flank but meeting with no French support, began to concentrate on evacuation of their forces. The Allies fell back on their only remaining port, Dunkirk.

Encouraged by Goering's boast that he could finish the remaining pocket of British and French forces from the air, Hitler halted his armour for two days, long enough to make defence against it possible. The population of South East England responded wonderfully to the challenge of danger and a mercifully calm sea. Every kind of fishing boat and pleasure craft ferried men from the beaches to waiting destroyers or back to British ports. Under relentless air attack, the British evacuated about 200,000 of their own troops and 139,000 French and Belgians.

Despite this setback, Hitler had much to be pleased with. The French attempted to defend along the Weygand Line of the Somme and the Aisne. The German armour met stiffer resistance than on the Meuse but again broke through. On June 14th Paris fell, undefended. Italy, anxious to join in the spoils, hurriedly attacked in the south. On June 22nd, the defeatist Marshal Pétain accepted the German terms of surrender in the same

Field Marshal Goering and his staff look across
from France towards the English cliffs, 1940

railway carriage in which the Germans had signed their surrender in 1918.
By the end of June, Hitler was enjoying his first tour of Paris as its conqueror.
France was restricted to a southern region based on a new capital at Vichy.

In six weeks, Hitler had achieved victories beyond even the hopes of his
generals. The German casualties in France had been less than those in
Poland. Scornful of the caution of his advisers, Hitler was convinced of his
military genius. He expected that Britain would realise her position and
seek terms for peace. The British had now as their leader Winston Churchill,
who had come to power as a result of dissatisfaction at Chamberlain's
handling of affairs in Norway. For the first time Hitler was faced with an
opponent who was his equal in ability to stir national emotions and also
possessed limitless amounts of the willpower to which Hitler attached so
much importance. There was no longer any talk of gentlemanly agree-

ments. In his first speech broadcast to the people, Churchill spoke of the Nazis as 'one of the foulest and most soul-destroying tyrannies'. He saw their defeat as vital to the cause of freedom and mankind. His message was a defiant 'We shall never surrender.' Despite this Hitler did not issue specific orders for the invasion of Britain until July 16th and was still offering peace in a speech to the Reichstag on July 19th.

Before invasion was possible, it was essential to German plans that they should control the air in order to protect their armada once it was afloat. Goering was confident of success. The British had 820 front line aircraft, the *Luftwaffe* 2,600. On August 12th the attack began, and by the 15th, 1,800 German aircraft were attacking a wide range of targets. The British were ready. Air Chief Marshal Sir Hugh Dowding had foreseen the battle and fought stubbornly to preserve enough fighters from the battle in France. Their pilots, joined by some equally skilled and brave Poles and Belgians who had escaped to England, proved to be well-trained and of matchless courage. The Hurricane fighter held its own with the Messerschmitt 109 and the Spitfire was the best of the three. Most important of all, an English scientist, A. F. Wilkins, had provided the idea of radar in 1934 and this had been developed by a team led by Sir Robert Watson-Watt. This discovery enabled the British to detect by radio waves the course and size of German attacks and concentrate their defences accordingly.

Nevertheless the battle was exceptionally fierce. Between the 15th and 23rd of August, although they suffered almost double the losses of the Royal Air Force, the *Luftwaffe* came near to permanently destroying the ring of airfields around London. On the 23rd, Churchill ordered a night retaliatory attack on Berlin. Hitler was furious and ordered an all-out assault on London. Although the English capital suffered fearful losses and many other industrial cities were bombed and burnt, the RAF had time to repair its airfields and British morale did not crack. In fact British bombers pounded the invasion craft assembled across the Channel, and on September 13th, they destroyed eighty large transports in Ostend alone. On September 17th, Hitler postponed his plans for invasion indefinitely. On October 12th Field Marshal Keitel issued a directive which stated that further attacks on England were simply to maintain political and military pressure. Germany had suffered her first defeat.

Although Hitler's plan to bring Britain to her knees had failed, he still had surprises in store for his generals. As early as July 29th, before the Battle of Britain began, Hitler had made up his mind to attack Russia. For a time his plans were known only to a few top commanders. Goering was not informed until November. Perhaps annoyed that the Russians had been busy annexing Baltic states while he was involved in the West, Hitler at some time in the summer decided to attack Russia, even if the British had not made peace. It became clear that Hitler's concern for 'Living Space' was still uppermost in his mind.

Hitler's plans for his attack on Russia were for a short while complicated by the behaviour of his ally. Having entered the war on 10th June 1940 hoping to make quick profits from the defeat of France, Mussolini was anxious to present Hitler with some new initiative of his own. The Germans had planned that the Italians should restrict their activities to an attack on the British in Egypt. This in fact proved more than enough to occupy them. Undeterred by lack of success and his commanders' warnings, on October 28th Mussolini ordered his troops to begin an attack on Greece. By the spring of 1941, the Italians were facing disaster. The British General O'Connor drove them out of Egypt and again out of Cyrenaica, the eastern province of Libya. The Italian colonies in East Africa were attacked and Mussolini's empire collapsed. The campaign in Greece went badly, and the Italians were forced to ask for German help.

Fully appreciating the importance of the Balkans to his plans in Russia, Hitler decided to invade Greece. For good measure he also invaded Yugoslavia, where a group of Yugoslav officers had rebelled against alliance with Germany. Both attacks began on April 6th 1941. German armour was still extremely formidable. Bombers pounded Belgrade. Within five days Yugoslavia was defeated. It took another fortnight to finish the Greeks. To add to Hitler's pleasure, the dispatch of Rommel, one of his best tank generals, to Libya had resulted in the British being pushed back into Egypt. The main result of his Balkan adventure seemed merely to have been the postponement of his attack on Russia from May 15th to June 22nd. The *Fuehrer* was confident the delay would not be important.

Throughout the previous winter the German forces had been building up in the East. By the time they attacked they had nearly 160 German, Finnish and Rumanian divisions, nineteen of them armoured and twelve motorised. The whole operation was covered by 2,700 aircraft. Hitler planned a three-pronged assault, aimed at vast encircling movements. He was confident that defeat would bring the Bolshevik government crumbling down, and he expected the campaign to last two months.

At first everything went wonderfully well. By July 16th the central

German force had reached Smolensk, 450 miles from its starting point. But from the beginning the Germans were surprised by the stubbornness of Russian resistance. Furthermore, in areas like the Ukraine where the Germans were at first greeted as liberators, the treatment of prisoners and the activities of the SS soon established indelible hatred. Stalin was able to present the war to his people as one of national survival. On 29th June he formed a Defence Committee to co-ordinate the war effort, and whole factories and their staffs were transported from the path of German invasion to the far side of the Urals. Still, for the time being the Germans made enormous advances. Hitler became excited by the prospect of encircling the Ukraine. On the central front 600,000 Russian prisoners were captured in two pockets. By November 27th the German tanks were halted only nineteen miles from Moscow. Some actually reconnoitred the suburbs.

The Russians then provided their thunderbolt. On December 5th, when even Hitler admitted the need to halt the advance due to the winter, the Russians began a massive counter-offensive. This had already begun near Rostov. However, the capture of Moscow would have compensated for this. To German amazement, the Russians reinforced the Moscow front with 100,000 men, 300 tanks and 2,000 guns. For the first time the Germans were on the defensive. Warmly-clad Russians were flung against exhausted German troops without winter clothing and threatened to break through. Hitler's reaction was characteristic. He saw the issue as one of willpower, and himself took over from Brauchitsch as Commander-in-Chief of the Army. All German forces were ordered to fight where they stood. Officers as high as Field Marshal von Rundstedt were relieved of their commands for disobedience. Thousands of Germans died in battle and from the cold, but the line held. Hitler was more than ever convinced of his genius.

Despite events in Russia, the Germans ended 1941 in confident mood. In November, Hitler had entertained ambassadors from Italy, Spain, Finland, Denmark and five Balkan states to the vision of a new European order. They were joined by a Japanese embassy and ceremoniously renewed the Anti-Comintern pact. On December 7th the alliance developed further. The Japanese made a surprise attack on the American fleet in Hawaii at Pearl Harbour. Hitler, having previously urged them to attack the British in Singapore, was delighted. He cheerfully announced that he joined them in war with the United States. The year which had begun with Britain as the only undefeated enemy ended with Germany at war with two major world powers.

◄ The Russian infantry at Stalingrad gave the
    Germans their first major defeat

10

Defeat
and Destruction

1942 began with a series of triumphs for Hitler and his allies, the Axis (or Central) powers. Having crippled the American Navy, the Japanese swept through South-East Asia. They drove the British out of Malaya. Singapore and Hong Kong fell into their hands. They were well on their way to capturing Burma. The Dutch were driven from their East Indies and the Americans from the Philippines. In the Atlantic, the United States was not yet able to protect its merchant shipping, and German U-boats wrought fearful damage. In the first three weeks of attack they sank 250,000 tons of shipping. In November they reached a climax of 800,000 tons. Meanwhile Hitler had reinforced Rommel in North Africa and launched a devastating air attack on Malta. In May Rommel began his offensive and within a month had captured Tobruk and entered Egypt. The British were driven back to El Alamein, only sixty miles from Alexandria.

The Germans, however, were mainly preoccupied with events in Russia. The summer campaign began well. The Russian attack launched in May and aimed at recapturing Kharkov was heavily defeated. The Russians lost over six hundred tanks and the Germans had superiority in armour of ten to one. On June 28th, Hitler ordered a great new offensive to begin. He repeated the mistakes of the year before. He underestimated Russian strength and split his forces. One thrust was aimed towards the Volga and

Stalingrad, the other towards the oilfields of the Caucasus. Through over-confidence, forces which could have captured Stalingrad in July were diverted to the Caucasus. The German line became greatly over-extended, while the greater part of the northern flank was protected by Italian, Hungarian and Rumanian troops.

The drive to the Caucasus was halted by the Russians. When the German generals tried to urge a halt in the attack to allow the reorganisation of forces, Hitler flew into a rage and again issued the order that no ground must be given. The attack on Stalingrad became more and more difficult. The Germans were obliged to engage in bitter house-to-house fighting in which tanks were of little value and the Russians were able to reduce war to man-to-man combat. The German Commander Paulus was offered promotion if he succeeded, and ordered an all-out assault on the Russian strongpoints: a factory, an ordnance plant and a steel works. The battle reached new intensity. A house might take fifteen days to capture. Dead covered factory floors. Russian machine-guns operated from unused ovens. Meanwhile, the Russians, commanded by Zhukov, built up forces to the north and south and prepared their trap.

On November 19th, Zhukov unleashed six fresh armies, 450 new tanks and an artillery barrage from over two thousand guns. By the evening of the 23rd, the Germans were encircled. The Russians further increased their fire power, and German relief forces could not break through or the *Luftwaffe* maintain supplies. On January 31st 1943 Paulus surrendered with the remains of 250,000 men. 130,000 Germans were directed to Russian prison cages. The *Fuehrer* had suffered a major catastrophe.

The year which had begun so well ended with a depressing prospect. In Asia the British at Ceylon and the Americans at Midway Island had inflicted their first defeats on the Japanese. On the night of May 30th, the RAF delivered their thousand-bomber raid on Cologne. Industrial towns all over Germany began to dread the night. Worst of all, one of Germany's great successes, Rommel, had met his match in Africa. On August 8th, the British Eighth Army came under the command of General Montgomery. He set about re-establishing morale by personal contact with his men, and then steadily built up a very powerful defensive position. Rommel was obliged to attack forces twice his size. Despite inflicting heavy losses on the British, Rommel's forces were just too few. The British had been reinforced by American Sherman tanks and enjoyed complete air superiority. The Panzer (mobile armour) Army was thrown into headlong retreat. The

British infantry capture a German tank in the desert, 1942

battle of El Alamein was fought between October 23rd and November 4th. Four days later the English and Americans landed in Morocco. The Germans were gradually trapped by an attack from both sides on Tunisia. The British and Americans controlled the sea and air. In May 1943 the Germans surrendered and another 25,000 men fell into Allied hands as prisoners-of-war.

By 1943 life in the German Reich was exceedingly grim. On the eve of war the SS had been built up to number 250,000 men. It was planned that they would form an *élite* inside Germany, dedicated to protect Nazism, and also maintain law and order in occupied territories. From the beginning their behaviour in war set new standards of horror. As soon as the Germans invaded Poland, the plans for redistributing populations and exploiting Jewish or Slav workers were put into effect. Mass shootings and the murder of prisoners through forced marches and starvation were commonplace. General Kluge received a letter which read, 'Last week I heard an 18½-year-old SS soldier, once a decent boy, say calmly that it was not exactly pleasant to machine-gun ditches filled with thousands of Jews and then throw earth on bodies which were still moving.' In the West, where comparatively humane standards were supposed to prevail, the random shooting of prisoners who had fought too well occurred frequently in 1940. When the Russian campaign began the next year, atrocities started at once. For the first five months, 100,000 Jews a month were massacred, mostly by machine-guns. They were made to lie in neat rows, sometimes on top of the newly dead, in order to speed up the killing. After the capture of Kharkov in the autumn, 100,000 civilians were machine-gunned into ditches which they had been forced to dig themselves. Hundreds of thousands of Russian prisoners were starved to death. Goering commented to Ciano, 'The Russian prisoners-of-war have started to eat each other. This year between twenty and thirty million people will die of hunger in Russia. Perhaps this is a good thing.'

Undoubtedly the worst atrocities occurred in Poland and Russia. However, extreme measures also occurred in occupied territories like France and Czechoslovakia. In September 1941 the famous 'Night and Fog' decree was issued, which ordered that those even suspected of sabotage should be arrested without the knowledge of their families and transported to Germany. At Oradour-sur-Glâne, three hundred men were shot and four hundred women and children burnt in a reprisal actually intended for nearby Oradour-sur-Vayres. In Lidice in Czechoslovakia, 172 men were shot to avenge the death of SS leader 'Hangman' Heydrich. Heydrich's obituary in the *Völkischer Beobachter* spoke of his 'generous determination to exchange trust for trust'.

The Jews were of course singled out for special treatment. As early as April 1941 Hitler had informed Goering and Himmler of his intention to exterminate all Jews under Nazi control. On January 20th 1942 Heydrich brought forward his plans for the 'final solution' of the Jewish problem. Jews were to be systematically deported to the East to forced labour and extermination camps. Mass killing techniques were perfected. New arrivals were stripped in preparation for a supposed shower. Soberly dressed musicians played light music to ease their filing into giant gas chambers able to hold up to 2,000 at a time. When the doors had been sealed, prussic acid crystals were dropped through the ventilation shafts. After a quarter of an hour, other Jews were forced to clean the dead bodies and collect valuables, including gold teeth, which were deposited in a special account at the Reichsbank. The slaughter was given a grisly twist by scientific experiments. Collections were made of skulls and other human parts. At Buchenwald the commandant's wife, Ilse Koch, selected tattooed skins to be made into lamp

shades. Doctors tried out the limits of human resistance to freezing and the rupture of lungs at high altitudes. An SS captain, Josef Kramer, on trial at Nuremberg after the war, stated, 'I had no feelings in carrying out these things . . . that was the way I had been trained.' Perhaps equally shocking are the letters from firms vying for the orders to manufacture gas chambers and cremation ovens, and boasting of their 'durability, use of the best material and faultless workmanship'. The claims were not vain. It is estimated that some five million Jews were systematically murdered.

The Germans themselves fared better in material terms. The plunder of conquered territories provided food and comfort unknown elsewhere in Europe. However, as early as the autumn of 1939 the number of crimes carrying the death penalty had increased to forty-six and included listening to foreign broadcasts and any anti-national act. While victory lasted Hitler recorded his successes in frequent speeches. After the defeats of 1942, information was more and more controlled by Goebbels. Criticism of the regime, however mild, became extremely dangerous. After March 1942, Albert Speer directed the German economy more and more rigorously towards war production. Thousands of conquered workers were driven into slave labour to feed the German war machine. The stench of the dead in towns like Weimar that were near concentration camps must have created its own type of terror.

Above all, the German civilian population began to live in greater and greater fear of Allied aerial bombing. The pressures of war stimulated the progress of scientific destruction. The Allies switched from attacks on industrial targets to an attempt to break civilian morale. The climax of this was the dreadful air raid on Dresden in February 1945 which killed more than 100,000 civilians. Perhaps the curious combination of official hopes for victory and individual experience of disaster is best illustrated by the manager of one of I. G. Farben's plants, who early in 1945 reported that although his plant was bombed out and occupied by the British Army, he was happy to forecast a five per cent dividend for the first quarter of 1945.

1943 was the year in which the Allied powers began to take the offensive against Germany. One of the decisive turning-points was the Battle of the Atlantic. The appalling losses at the hands of the U-boats required strenuous counter-attack. The Americans were converted to the idea of escorted convoys. New radar equipment enabled the location of U-boats. High-frequency direction-finders were developed to locate radio signals. In the spring of 1943 some long-range Liberator aircraft were released to provide

◄ Dr Klein, senior doctor at Belsen, among some
of the camp's victims after the Allied liberation

German dead abandoned in the retreat from Russia

full air cover. Finally escort aircraft carriers allowed the Allies to seek out and pursue attackers. In May 1943 forty-one U-boats were destroyed. In September the German Admiral Doenitz was able to retaliate with a new acoustic torpedo that fastened on to the sound of the propellers of a ship. The Allies responded with the 'foxer' noise-maker that diverted the torpedo. By March 1944 the Germans had in practice conceded defeat. Not only was this a triumph for the British Navy and Air Force, but now ever-increasing American supplies could be channelled into Europe to prepare for the attack on the European mainland.

In July 1943, British and American forces from North Africa and Malta invaded Sicily. Six weeks later, they invaded the mainland. The opponents of Mussolini took him captive and a new Italian government under Marshal Badoglio offered the Allies an armistice. The way into Europe seemed open. But the German commander in Italy, Kesselring, reacted very promptly. The Germans exploited the ideal defensive nature of the peninsula and despite attempts to by-pass their defences by an amphibious landing at Anzio, the struggle for Italy was hard-fought and bitter.

The largest German forces were still concentrated on the Russian front. In July 1943, the Russians held the German attacks on the central Kursk front and brought forward enormous reinforcements from their Ural industrial complex. They were also aided by the arrival of crucial supplies by convoys in the North from the United States, Britain and Canada. These convoys had to fight their way round Norway, battling equally with German U-boats, battle cruisers, appalling weather and icy seas. The arrival of thousands of American supply vehicles greatly assisted the Russian advance. Their trump card was nevertheless massive numbers and supplies. They amazed the Germans with counter-offensives along the full range of their fronts. By August 23rd they had regained Kharkov, by September 25th Smolensk, on November 6th Kiev. The Germans counter-attacked and checked the advance for a time, but in December the Russians attacked again, this time in a winter offensive. In 1944 Russian war production reached new heights: 29,000 tanks and self-propelled guns, 40,000 aircraft, 122,000 pieces of artillery according to official figures. Although the Germans and their allies had over 4,000,000 men, the Russian Red Army numbered 6,425,000. Again an offensive was delivered in a series of crushing blows all along the front. On July 17th, the Russians could parade 57,000 German prisoners through the streets of Moscow, and the Germans admitted losses in the three months from June of 917,000 men. By the end of the year the Russians had reached the Baltic on a wide front and were threatening East Prussia.

Apart from the disasters on the Eastern Front, the German military situation was rapidly deteriorating elsewhere. In Italy, the Allies under General Alexander launched an offensive in May. At long last the remains of the monastery of Monte Cassino, which the Germans had converted into an almost impregnable fortress, were captured. Contact was established with the Anzio beachhead. On June 4th, Rome was liberated.

Two days later, the long-awaited assault in France began. The Supreme Allied Commander, General Eisenhower, through his skill as a co-ordinator, forged together the greatest international invasion force ever known. The Allies first pounded German supply routes and strategic bridges from the air. Then over 4,000 ships and landing craft ferried across 156,000 men and 20,000 vehicles to the bay of the Seine between Caen and the Cherbourg peninsula. The Allies were fortunate to possess a wonderful range of technical aids, tanks that could make pathways through minefields, lay tracks, construct bridges and even tanks that could swim. They were mainly the achievement of Major-General Hobart, who had personally been rescued by Churchill from premature retirement as a corporal in the Home Guard. Only on the Omaha Beach where the American General Bradley refused their help to the dreadful cost of his men, did Hobart's 'Funnies' fail to secure remarkably successful landings.

Enjoying total air superiority, the Allies built up strong supplies of arms and men, profiting from the help of artificially constructed harbours. Rommel organised a swift response. Seven out of his eight Panzer divisions kept the British pinned down in Caen. This gave the Americans the opportunity to break out. On July 31st General Patton's tanks poured South and West into Brittany. The front suddenly became mobile and extensive. The Americans fought off a Panzer attack ordered by Hitler, and then their left wing joined with the Canadian First Army to trap 50,000 German prisoners in the 'Falaise pocket' inside their pincer movement. By September the British forces had thrust north-east towards Brussels and Antwerp. The Germans, pressed on two fronts, were in a critical position.

By July, the German military leaders were determined to try to persuade Hitler to admit defeat. Rommel urged Hitler to offer the withdrawal of German forces to the Reich in exchange for the stopping of the air raids. He was probably saved from a summary fate by being badly wounded by an aircraft while travelling in an open car. On July 20th Colonel Stauffenberg placed a time bomb in a briefcase under the table at which Hitler was conducting a military conference at his headquarters in East Prussia. As it was a warm day, Hitler had moved his conference from his concrete bunker to a wooden hut. The briefcase was moved at a crucial moment. The bomb exploded, killed some officers, but not Hitler. Had it gone off in the confined space of the bunker, everyone would have been killed. Stauffenberg, seeing the explosion, hurriedly flew to Berlin to organise a *coup* and the disarming of the SS and Gestapo. But then Hitler's survival became known and the *coup* collapsed. Fortunate leaders like Stauffenberg were allowed by friendly superiors to shoot themselves. The rest, plus anyone who was subject to Hitler's or Himmler's suspicions, were hounded down and murdered. A Field Marshal, three generals and four other officers were slowly hanged with piano wire. A film of the hanging was made on Hitler's orders. Altogether at least 4,980 people were executed. Rommel was allowed the chance to commit suicide and given a State funeral. The Nazi salute became compulsory for all Army officers.

Although Hitler placed his hopes on some new V1 and V2 rockets, by the

American troops land in Normandy, June 6th 1944

end of 1944 the German position was hopeless. The Allied armies captured the rocket launching sites. The Germans could still show surprising determination. General Model, transferred from the Russian front, organised a remarkable rally in the West in September and October 1944. An Allied airborne attack at Arnhem was bloodily crushed. In mid-September the Germans launched a last desperate offensive in the Ardennes. Exploiting surprise and mist and rain which prevented air attack, the Fifth and Sixth Panzer Armies for a time threw the Americans into confusion, but they were never broken. Montgomery swung his reserves south to face the thrust. The attack petered out and ended with a skilful withdrawal. The Germans had fatally engaged their last reserves.

In February 1945, the Allied leaders met at a conference in Yalta in the Crimea and made the plans for victory. The frontiers of Poland were defined. The Americans promised to halt their advance at Czechoslovakia. In March 1945 the Allies crossed the Rhine and the Russians poured into Germany from Poland. The German Army began to surrender at around

The price of German defeat. The devastation of Dresden after Allied bombing

10,000 men a day and seemed mainly concerned to ensure that the Americans and British forestalled the Russian advance as much as possible. Hitler moved to his bunker in Berlin. He was joined by only a few of his most fanatical friends, including Goebbels and his family. The Nazi Party Leader Martin Bormann decided what could be told to the *Fuehrer* as he conjured with imaginary forces to achieve a final counter-stroke. The American President Roosevelt's death in April was grasped as a miraculous deliverance. His last army, a few remnants plus some of the fifteen-year-old boys and sixty-year-old men whom Hitler had called for a final stand, was led by General Wenck to seek safety in surrender to the Americans.

On April 25th the Russian armies surrounded Berlin. For five days bitter battles still raged in the streets of the city. On April 29th Hitler decided to marry Eva Braun, who had been his long-suffering mistress for more than twelve years. A registrar was found to perform the ceremony according to Nazi rites. Hitler then spent several hours dictating his will in which he laid responsibility for the war on 'the agents of international Jewry'. A small

wedding reception was held. Bormann and Goebbels were joined by Hitler's staff to drink a glass of champagne. The next day Hitler said good-bye to Goebbels and his wife. He then withdrew with Eva Braun and they died together by revolver and cyanide at 3.35 p.m.

By the time that the Russians had hoisted their Red Flag over the Chancellery, all that was left of Hitler were his charred remains, burnt on his own orders. Goebbels had boasted at his last news conference, 'When we leave, the earth will tremble.' The day after the *Fuehrer's* death, Goebbels arranged his own and his family's. Himmler and Goering were also later to seek oblivion through suicide.

The quest for living space and a new order had ended with foreign armies meeting in the Fatherland. The industrial might of Germany lay in rubble. Over four million Germans had been sacrificed in battle. Of those that remained, very few would ever admit to having been a Nazi.

11
The Rebuilding of Germany

The Allies had been united by the desire to destroy Hitler's Germany. By the Potsdam Agreement of August 1945, they took over the government of Germany which was divided into four zones, each under the control of a military governor, with Berlin as a four-power island in the Russian zone. The victims of Nazi aggression were compensated for their losses. Territory east of the Oder and Neisse rivers was given to the Poles. Russia regained Estonia, Latvia and Lithuania as well as slices of East Prussia, pre-war Poland, Rumania and Czechoslovakia. Czechoslovakia herself regained the territory lost to Hitler at Munich and expelled from it three and a half million Germans. As Stalin said in 1945, 'The century-old struggle between Slav and German has ended in victory for the Slavs.' Fearful of the implications of this, twelve million refugees fled from the Russian zone into the ruined territories run by America, Britain and France.

Only the Russians in fact knew clearly what they wanted from Germany. The 'Hitlerite' class structure in the Russian zone was dismantled. They confiscated all estates over 250 acres, nationalised the banks and insurance companies and most of industry. The Socialist Unity Party led by Communists established a monopoly of political power. Russian tanks crushed a desperate revolt in 1953. Some concentration camps lived on in East

British   American   French   Soviet   Polish

**THE ALLIED ZONES OF ADMINISTRATION AND THE DIVISION
OF GERMANY AFTER THE SECOND WORLD WAR**

Germany as part of the thirty-two 'labour camps' that correct the politically
unreliable. War booty was systematically directed to Russia.

In the West, American initiative has led to the creation of the strongest
economic force in Europe. As early as 1946, the American Secretary of
State, James F. Byrnes, began to talk of the necessity for German recovery.
In January 1947, the Americans and British fused into a Bi-Zone. In June
1948, the three Western Powers introduced a new currency into their
sectors, the Deutsche Mark. In six months production doubled. The
Russians refused to co-operate and introduced their own currency reform.
They went on to introduce a full-scale economic blockade of Berlin. The
Western Powers responded with the Airlift of one plane every four minutes
to bring supplies into Berlin, which indicated their refusal to let Berlin
become a Russian hostage.

In May 1949 the Western Powers faced up to the logic of a divided

Germany and set up the Federal Republic. In October the Russians responded with the Democratic Republic of East Germany.

In the Federal Republic, a parliament was elected and also a Federal Chancellor, Konrad Adenauer. Adenauer's outstanding characteristic was the ability to concentrate all Germany's energies on her practical needs, without being haunted by the past. He saw West Germany's future as inevitably involved politically and economically with the West. Under his guidance Germany entered into schemes for economic union, the European Coal and Steel Community in 1952 and the European Economic Community by the Treaty of Rome in 1957. In 1954 West Germany restored its military position by joining the North Atlantic Treaty Organisation, avowedly formed for protection against Russian attack. The policy was a brilliant success. The German 'Economic Miracle' made her by 1960 the third strongest economic power in the world behind America and Russia. Symbolic of her new wealth and position was the payment of eleven million dollars as compensation to returning Jews and the payment of three million marks to the new state of Israel.

The economic progress of the Federal Republic and the steady drain of some two million refugees, often highly qualified, from East to West led on the night of August 12–13th 1961 to the building of the Berlin Wall, perhaps now destined to be the permanent stark symbol of a divided Germany. It has, however, led to the Democratic Republic experiencing its own economic leap forward and developing the highest income per head in Eastern Europe and a chemical industry second only in production to the Americans.

Happily 1969 was not only a year in which the Deutsche Mark was revalued with an increase of 9·29 per cent, but also one in which Germany elected its first Social Democrat President, Dr Gustav Heinemann. Furthermore, his election, like that of his Social Democrat Chancellor, Herr Willi Brandt, was orderly and directly associated with the success of a republic.

BOOKS FOR FURTHER READING

BALFOUR, Michael, *The Kaiser and His Times* (London, 1964)

BULLOCK, Alan, *Hitler: a Study in Tyranny* (London, 1952)

CARSTEN, F. L., *The Reichwehr and Politics* (London, 1966)

DEMETER, Karl, *The German Officer Corps* (London, 1965)

EYCK, Erich, *History of the Weimar Republic*, 2 vols. (London, 1962 and 1964)

HITLER, Adolf, *Mein Kampf* (London, 1939)

KEYNES, J. M., *The Economic Consequences of the Peace* (London, 1919)

MANN, Golo, *The History of Germany since 1789* (London, 1968)

MEINECKE, Friedrich, *The German Catastrophe* (Harvard University Press, 1950)

SHIRER, William L., *The Rise and Fall of the Third Reich* (London, 1960)

TAYLOR, A. J. P., *The Course of German History* (London, 1945)

—— *The Struggle for Mastery in Europe* (London, 1954)

—— *Bismarck* (London, 1955)

TREVOR-ROPER, H., *The Last Days of Hitler* (London, 1947, 2nd ed. 1950)

WHEELER-BENNETT, J. W., *The Nemesis of Power* (London, 1953)

Index